Gloria Needlman, Ed.D.

It's Not Forsythia, It's For Me

My Years Teaching Young Children

ARCHWAY
PUBLISHING

Archway Publishing books may be ordered through booksellers or by contacting:

Archway Publishing
1663 Liberty Drive
Bloomington, IN 47403
www.archwaypublishing.com
1 (888) 242-5904

Because of the dynamic nature of the Internet, any web addresses or links contained in this book may have changed since publication and may no longer be valid. The views expressed in this work are solely those of the author and do not necessarily reflect the views of the publisher, and the publisher hereby disclaims any responsibility for them.

ISBN: 978-1-4808-3840-6 (sc)
ISBN: 978-1-4808-3841-3 (e)

Library of Congress Control Number: 2016916954

Print information available on the last page.

Archway Publishing rev. date: 11/04/2016

Contents

Introduction

For over forty years my professional life was spent interacting with young children, learning about them as I facilitated their learning. I was delighted being a student teacher, disliked being a substitute, learned a great deal in my early teaching positions and absolutely loved the thirty four years I taught at the University of Chicago Laboratory Schools. Now an octogenarian, my role with children continues in new and different ways, though I have been retired from a classroom for well over a decade. I have been involved with and for young children in experiences I want remembered and reused. I feel these stories are worthy of the paper they utilize.

In my personal life, my husband and I married sixty-six years ago and have three adult kids and a granddaughter. I was a stay-at-home mother until our youngest child was ready for school and my professional journey at the Laboratory Schools began.

More Than Book Learning

From my undergraduate years some significant words of wisdom stayed with me. *"Imagine this is the only day a child will ever have in school. Make it important and meaningful."* This powerful message made me strive to have some special contact, an important happening for each child every day. I admit it wasn't always possible, though there was always time for a hug, a positive word, a pat on the head before the day ended.

I never forgot the lesson delivered by another professor who, while standing on top of his desk spoke to our undergraduate class. We strained our heads, stretched our necks trying to see his face as he stood so high above us. I certainly have no recollection of what his actual words were, but his crazy demonstration, his unspoken message taught me that to little children, adults appear just as he appeared—mostly knees. I knew I had to get down on the floor and make eye contact with the youngsters I'd one day be teaching. The holes worn in many of my slacks are proof that I NEVER forgot this message as much of each day, for over thirty years, I was on the floor making face to face contact.

My teaching was influenced by words of wisdom that came from many sources. A strong message came from a speech by Mahatma Gandhi. *"You must be the change you wish to see in the world."* These words helped me decide what age-group of children I wanted to teach. Reaching the youngest children in their first school experiences could make a difference. Now in my retirement years I want to believe I may indeed have made some changes, though possibly only in small ways.

Today, decades later, I remain in contact with many of the children I taught. They are now adults who hold meaningful, even powerful positions as educators, doctors, writers, scientists and artists, though I have no idea of what or where many of them are today. Not every child who sat on my lap, laughing, sometimes crying or needing to tell me something very important, can I count as a success story. I do know of those who are making changes in the world and I like to think I played a role in their lives as I instilled a love of learning, of being curious, of seeking answers as their long educational road was launched under my wings.

In 2010, fifteen years after I was awarded the *Kohl McCormick Early Childhood Teaching Award*, I was completely taken by surprise at the yearly Teacher Education Awards lunch when the mistress of ceremonies, Merri Dee, explained to a huge audience of educators, administrators, and community activists, that in order to show what influence an award winner of the past had on a former student a past award winner's student was to be called to the stage to thank the teacher who inspired her. She then described this unnamed person—"a graduate of Harvard University and Northwestern Law School, the recipient of the National Endowment for the Arts, author of five children's book and one memoir, and a former Nursery/ Kindergarten student" but before she could say more I recognized the person being described. I jumped up from my chair and called out her name, and at the very same time my name was called. With the most complimentary words Merri Dee briefly spoke of how, during my thirty four years of teaching, I helped develop a large number of great minds, and this former student, one of those great minds, was indeed my now grownup, Natasha Tarpley.

I don't know how I was able to reach the stage, and without a thought in my head, Natasha and I hugged. As I gained some composure, Tasha spoke these incredible words:

"One of my favorite poets, Lucille Clifton, wrote, '…happen you will rise and learn to forget the geography of fixed things; happen you walk past all of the places you meant to stay and wonder at the way, it seemed so marvelous to move.' To me, this quote sums up education the preparation, the gift that I was given by having Gloria Needlman as my teacher."

As I listened to my once little student I thought, here was living proof that in some way I may have touched on Gandhi's message.

Now move back in time, over sixty years, to what and who helped shape the teacher I became. Undergraduate courses were certainly meaningful; however it was my practicum in my senior year in a wonderful Nursery School classroom at the Laboratory Schools that confirmed what I thought schools should be. I wanted to teach at *that* school because what I was exposed to as a student teacher felt so right to me about education and little children. Though I was not yet married, it was my dream that if I had children, when they were of school age I'd become a University of Chicago Laboratory Schools teacher, and however many children I parented would be Lab School students.

Growing a Resume

Following my college graduation I began building my resume before applying for a position at the University of Chicago Laboratory Schools. I became certified to teach in the Chicago Public Schools which I did as a substitute in various grade levels; I held part-time teaching jobs, all the while gaining experience and confidence.

It was the director of a cooperative nursery school in one of my first teaching positions, who, when interacting with parents, children, or the teaching staff, neglected to make eye contact or give her full attention to what was asked or said to her. During that year I encountered her minimal involvement and decided to NEVER do as she did. Later on I thought of this as negative teaching as it was very important as it taught me what NOT to do.

Ours was a Lab School Family

In time, I become a mother, and my early dream actually came to fruition. When our youngest child was to enter first grade and our others to be in fourth and seventh grades, the four of us applied to Lab. I am thrilled to say, we each filled the necessary requirements and were all accepted. I was hired to team teach in a two year Nursery class for three and four year olds and our three children were assigned to their proper grades. My husband and I attended ever so many parent teacher conferences, to say nothing of the years that I packed our food for end of the year picnics held for Nursery, Lower, Middle and High School families.

Over the span of thirty-four years, I taught various programs having children with me for two years of Nursery School as well as two years in my combined Nursery/Kindergarten class. I also taught third grade to convince myself that with specific subject matter to be covered I was the right teacher. I taught children and then subject matter. My last year, before retiring, was a one year only-kindergarten class. Through my stories I recall happenings, events, projects, families, children and colleagues from many different years and many different settings at Lab. I trust you'll find them rich, innovative, exciting, or at the very least interesting.

Before teaching third grade I enrolled in a math class at the University, having realized it would be a good idea to tackle learning something I found to be difficult since we adults ask this of children regularly. I struggled to understand much of the material presented. I painfully learned this was an essential component to being a compassionate teacher. To work at mastery of a subject or concept that seems impossibly difficult can be a huge challenge. For me, and for the children I would teach, repetition, time, and extra help would be required for success along with, of course, much sincere encouragement. I knew I couldn't experience firsthand everything that I would ask of children, but this was certainly an eye opener that helped me be more aware and sensitive.

From a seemingly unimportant happening I gained a different empathetic insight. This took place the day I tripped on an unforgiving cement sidewalk and landed on both knees. Though I carefully washed and applied bandages, it hurt. I was in pain. Maybe every teacher and parent should at some time in his/her adult life fall down and scrape a body part. Too often we tell children their bruises will be better soon and stop hurting, maybe not. Those bruises I experienced from my fall took time, and led me to be more compassionate and understanding of the pains children encounter, be they from scrapes, bruises, frustrations, or hurt feelings.

As a teacher of little children, I knew a sympathetic ear wasn't enough. A wounded child required something more. After carefully checking the hurt area, doing the cleaning and bandaging, I'd ask the crying child, most often seated on my lap, to tell me her/his favorite song and together we would sing it three times. Magically, as the singing ended, the pain subsided and the child was able to feel good enough to jump down and resume activities. Involving singing and the time it took for three repetitions seemed the key to relief and acted as a significant help in many tough situations. While we sang, other children came to watch, listen, and sometimes to sing with us—each knowing if they needed help, I'd be there for them.

Being a Student Never Ends

My life was full as were my days and nights. During the day I was a teacher, but evenings I was a wife and a parent, and I traded hats when I once again became a student. I enrolled in a two year graduate program at the Chicago Institute for Psychoanalysis which proved to be extremely important as it greatly influenced my thinking and my teaching. The Teacher Education Program connected the work of teaching with the work of psychoanalysis. The program, conceived of by a brilliant woman, Kay Field, involved classes taught by psychoanalysts and social workers who exposed me and twelve other practicing teachers to insightful ways to think about children, learning and parents. During these years of night school I read the writings of Piaget, Erickson, Eckstein, Anthony, and others whose works I might never have found time to study on my own. Those writings, class discussions and projects added much to my understanding of the children I taught. For example I learned to carefully observe children and through my well-documented observations I was able to interact in more meaningful ways with the children and their parents as I gained insights and understanding of their behaviors.

During my teaching years I also enrolled in evening and summer classes at Erickson Institute and at Loyola University. I attended professional conferences across the country as a workshop attendee and as a workshop leader. The idea of not being a student and learning while teaching never entered my mind.

I earned my doctorate after I retired. It was important to me and was something I always wanted to pursue, but was unable to find the time and it did require time. It took me three years to complete the required class work and almost that long for my research and the writing of my dissertation, *A Behavioral Study of Young Children's Involvements in a Hands-on Museum*, which I defended while seated at my kitchen table on a conference call with my doctoral committee. My timing was in the wake of the 9/11 World Trade Center attack making it impossible to fly to the University in California. My research done at the Chicago Children's Museum was very meaningful as it reinforced the way I had always set up my classrooms to function—a safe place for discovery, learning and creativity.

I very seldom use my hard-earned Ed.D. initials but in retirement when I became Adjunct Faculty at a local college supervising *Teach for America* young people in very difficult inner city schools, I'd introduce myself as Dr. Needlman. I hoped my newly-earned title would give me a stronger position when meeting with principals to suggest ways to support the young inexperienced teachers. Though they were college graduates, they were not education majors, and their *Teach for America* training was only over six weeks during the summer before they were assigned to inner city schools.

Sorry to say, even with those initials, I wasn't successful in gaining real support from any of the principals for these young teachers in their day to day classroom work. They were promised mentors who were not available, no guidance or help was present, the materials in their rooms were inadequate, the class size was unmanageable—to say the schools I was involved with would have challenged even an experienced teacher is hardly a strong enough statement. As their supervisor, I only met a few times each month with each inexperienced teacher, hardly enough time to do the job I was hired to do. Of the five teachers I worked with, only one extended his contract and made a commitment to continue on making teaching his career. I reflected on my own teacher training and there was no comparison.

So much of my learning came from formal education, but some came from gut feelings. I must describe one lesson not taught in any class but spoken by a friend, an educational therapist who helped me to understand what I was unable to recognize. In discussing an upsetting conversation I had with a colleague she said, "Gloria, how would you resolve a similar situation between two of your little students?" I realized without any hesitation I knew instantly how to handle my adult conversation which had seemed impossibly difficult. Her simple comment made me understand my interpersonal relationships were not really different from those I competently dealt with children on a daily basis. I could have told my colleague that her words were hurtful and that when she could speak to me in a more respectful way, I would gladly respond. What a lesson to learn! The conflicts between children and conflicts between adults can be resolved in much the same way—with objectivity, with taking time to think before reacting and when reacting making sure to do so with honesty and integrity. John Dewey, the founder of the Laboratory Schools over a hundred years ago said, *"Failure is instructive. The person who really thinks learns quite as much from his failures as from his successes."*

Acknowledgements

I began this book almost ten years ago, but it could never have been completed without the help of my first-born son, Michael, who became my advisor, my editing partner, and my support when the computer and I couldn't get along and when I became discouraged that I would ever complete it. My friends, colleagues, family Carla Spann, Natasha Tarpley, Mary Wonderlick, Muriel Rogers. Julia Needlman who gave me encouragement and help as I struggled to find the way to present my years in classrooms working and living with young children, and I am grateful to them. Needless to say, my husband Allen was always involved with my classrooms and has encouraged me over these long years to stop other projects and get to writing. Though I was technically retired, I was so involved in gardening, in social justice work, in political action, that finding writing time was never easy, and the computer was often impossible.

Getting Started

Once in my Lab School classroom, I began each year a bit differently—it kept me on my toes and made me stop and reevaluate what I wanted to accomplish with each group of children. The years my class was made up of Nursery School children who would be with me for two years, I invited parents to the classroom on an evening before the opening day of school. My sole purpose was to answer any of their questions and concerns, and alleviate any anxieties especially for those whose firstborn children were to begin school. What a family milestone! I found often the turnout at this meeting was small with only a handful of parents attending, but no matter the size of the group, this casual evening provided a smooth beginning for the adults and helped to make a smooth beginning for their children. Their questions ranged from "My child is not always comfortable using a toilet, how do you handle wet clothing?" Or, "When my child is in the room, I really want to visit and see what is happening. Do I have to make an appointment before I stop in?" Mostly they were simple questions to answer and reassuring answers relieved some of the anxieties parents felt. If some concerns required privacy I set up another time for us to talk.

With other classes, during the summer, I'd mail a welcome postcard to each new child. On it I printed something about a piece of equipment or an area to be found in the classroom — e.g.

the place for making things and painting, the area with blocks, the trucks and small dolls, or the dress up clothes in the dramatic play area. On each card I wrote about puzzles and wonderful books they'd find in their school room. On the first day many a child entered clutching a worn out, well handled post card, looking for something I had written about and heading right for it. If I were still teaching today I might send an email or post some welcome words on my Facebook page. Contact methods may have changed, but I am certain helping children adjust hasn't.

The years I taught a combined Nursery and Kindergarten classroom, before school officially began, I invited the Kindergarten children—those entering our school from other Nursery Schools along with the 5-year-olds who had not attended any preschool program, and those now five who had been my Nursery kids and knew our classroom and its teachers—to a tanbark spreading party. (Tanbark is a type of soft ground covering material which we used for our school playground). My invitation to these families was to come to school on an August evening at 7:00 pm, an unusual time for youngsters to come to school, but this was a "work event".

As families arrived in the play yard they found bags of tanbark piled in stacks of sacks. We adults spaced the bags around the yard and opened them. The children, ready to be kindergarteners, used small rakes to spread the bark and create a new, fresh covering for their outdoor play space. Children who had not seen each other over the long summer vacation were delighted to meet and greet one another, and for new children, the unknown children new to Lab, this was a great introduction to their classmates and to the space that would be their play yard, making it comfortable and familiar. The ownership in taking care of the out-door area was part of the plan, and so year after year we relieved the custodial workforce of this chore, and children took over while having a great time replenishing the play-yard ground cover. It felt so right to have the group of Kindergarten children do something very special, and do it before the first opening days of school. Lemonade and popcorn certainly helped make it a great party.

At the start of each of my Nursery School years, I gradually introduced children to their new larger world. It was, for many, the first time they were on their own, away from home, exposed to and experiencing other non-family children, and having new adults care for them. I set up the class room to be challenging and inviting, but not overwhelming. As children entered on their first day after being warmly welcomed, they looked around, usually while holding onto their adult, and were asked to do two things:

> To select their cubby (the place to keep outdoor clothing),

AND

> To choose a mailbox (their own container that fit in an open cabinet).

These two spaces were identified with both a photo and the child's name card. As I watched the looks on faces, I was certain having a named place in our classroom was a good thing.

Children found the shelves that held games and toys to challenge cooperative play invited their participation, but if these things weren't appealing, they were encouraged to get involved with the large building blocks, or settle down comfortable with books that were possibly new to them and filled with illustrations. The art and writing materials, simple puzzles, games, and the dramatic play area beckoned boys and girls to enjoy and pretend. The room was certainly different for those first days as I set out just a sampling of the great supply of wonderful items I had in cabinets and closets. Once I knew this group of children as the school year progressed, the children's interest would motivate the changes in what materials were made available and together we'd build our classroom.

Some of the unusual toys and art materials I made available for play were from the community recycling center even though I was provided with an adequate budget—I was a teacher who loved to scrounge in weird places to find wonderful challenging play materials. The discarded hospital TV channel remotes were used by "airline pilots" and "garbage people" in ways I'd never dreamed were possible. An actual cone discarded from the Geophysics department became a Spaceship sparked by children's interests. (More about this later.)

Those first days of school involved making certain that adults and children were comfortably able to separate. For some this required extra support from me, for some it meant an adult stayed a short or a longer time, and there were some parents who found it harder to say good-bye than did their youngsters. I firmly insisted no adult was to ever just disappear without making eye contact with her/his child before leaving.

One parent reinforced for me the importance of tone and words used when speaking to youngsters. This mom's positive language became a model I often shared with parents, nannies, whoever was leaving a child at the beginning of school or on a particularly unsettled morning.

> Mrs. G. brought her twin boys to my classroom on their first morning and after walking from area to area with them in hand she picked up Stephan and then Victor, kissed them solidly and said, "Cheerio boys, you will have a wonderful morning and I will be back for you in time for lunch." There was no hesitation in her voice, no possibility that they might misunderstand what she said, and the boys smiled and moved on to find the blocks, the trucks, and the art easels. From that first separation day they easily threw a kiss, and entered the classroom each morning seemingly anticipating a great day.

Another parent's goodbye was not only hesitant but she used words that made her child upset. It took two weeks for this little girl, Anna, to comfortably be in school. Mother first kissed her little one goodbye, but stayed, making no move to leave. She told Anna she had no need to be afraid to be in school all alone. Anna certainly picked up the message. Instead of Mother comfortably leaving on that first day, with her daughter clinging to her skirt, sobbing they walked out of the room together. That evening I phoned Mother and made some suggestions as to how she could make the separation happen, but this same scene was repeated on the second day. On day three there was no change though I once again gently suggested Mother sit on the chair and encourage her daughter to move off and find the paints or blocks. Gradually, by the end of the first week, Mother was able to leave for an hour, but hurriedly returned to resume her close scrutiny of her daughter. I was never sure if she had to be convinced that her little girl was being cared for, or if her child really required her supportive presence. Finally, and it took two weeks, Mom was comfortable to leave when Anna, off to wash dolls in the water table, threw her a quick goodbye kiss. An active, involved life at school had begun for Anna.

Years later, Anna, grown up, became the guidance counselor at an independent school and hired me to help with admissions screening. We talked about her beginning school years, and clearly her mother had done many right things for her.

I remember a time when I spoke out to another adult in a forceful way, a change from my typical gentler manner of addressing someone unknown to me. I felt it was essential that I not be quiet and accepting but protective of the children who were always my first concern. This is what took place:

David's grandfather strolled into the classroom while most of the children were settled on their blankets for a resting time. He held a cigar in his mouth and in a bold voice announced his name and walked right in. (David had told me he'd be visiting, and we had anticipated his arrival, but much earlier in the day.) His abrupt, noisy entry disturbed several of the children who suddenly sat up from their resting postures. I gently took Grandfather by the arm, ushered him out of the room and into the hall. I introduced myself and asked that he first dispose of his cigar in a dish I offered and I then suggested that he would be more comfortable having a seat in the office or in the library for fifteen minutes. On his return, David would be ready to show him all around the classroom and introduce him to his friends. I explained that there were things that were not acceptable in my classroom and that he had already found two of them. He told me I was a gutsy female and he admired that. Exactly fifteen minutes later, he returned to the room with a less pompous attitude, and he and David enjoyed their time together. My classroom was for children. It was their place to feel safe and where caring for them was always of foremost importance for me.

A pet peeve of mine was hearing adults answer for their child rather than allowing the child to respond. I saw this behavior as disrespecting the child's ability to speak for her/him self with his own thoughts and words. I would step in and say, "Please let your son answer." Guess I was the gutsy female David's grandfather encountered whenever I felt a need to step up and support a child.

Many times every day children were exposed to letters and their sounds. Names were printed on drawings and children learned to recognize who was the artist. I'd call out a letter and children whose first name began with it would stand up. Or I'd say, "If your last name begins with 'O' it's your turn to go." All of us loved rhyming so I'd spout silly ones anytime, any place—"Three minutes more and we'll meet at the door." "Please take a seat. It's time that we meet." I'd use names, words and even nonsense syllables and play with them. "Smarty Marty, come to our party." Annie Bannanie, Fanny, Granny. Whenever there was an opportunity to spell a word, rhyme a name, play with sounds, we did it.

On the beginning days of the year, mailboxes were randomly chosen by each child with his/her name fastened to it and placed in a space in the cabinet that held four rows with six divided spaces in each row. Children and parents knew from day one that anyone could put things in a box, but only the child whose name appeared on it could take things out.

After just a few weeks into the school year, at rug time, I complained to my class about having a difficult time finding Justin's or Grace's mailbox. I questioned if there was a way the boxes might be arranged so that I, or anyone else, could easily locate a particular mailbox.

I was told, *"Just remember where the names are,"* *"Ask a kid to find her/his box,"* and then a child said, *"You could put them the way the alphabet goes."* This idea sounded good to me and no one objected though I was certain many had no idea of what that meant. Children then figured out the cabinet first had to be emptied, so each child removed her/his box and sat with it on the floor.

The first spaces were to be filled with the boxes of kids with names that began with the letter "A" those of Amy, Arthur and Alex. This created another problem. Which "A" name should come first, which one was second and which one third? It was finally suggested, and agreed by some, not all, that it was important to look beyond the first letter of each name—the second letter had to be looked at too. Finally Alex, Amy and Arthur put their boxes in Row 1, and when the row was filled children began to place the next boxes in Row 2. (Boxes were placed from the left to the right--the way needed to train children's eyes for reading—why miss an opportunity for learning). By the time the "S" names were reached, and there were five of them, almost every child seemed to understand that just using the first letter was not adequate, they had to look at the second and for some names even to the third letter to put them in alphabetical order — (Sara, Stanley, Steve, then Stuart, and finally Suzie) and as the last child placed his box in the open space, there were empty spaces, leaving one for each of our two teachers, and an extra one which later became the "Dead Letter Box."

Because every child was involved, almost everyone was able to wait to replace her/his bin, even though it was a longer rug time than usual.

Mailboxes not only involved the alphabet but also numbers. I explained I now had an address for my box and that it was 4E, and that Mrs. S's, an assistant teacher address was 4F. Some children looked completely confused while there were some who figured it out and either raised their hands or just shouted out their addresses. The address for Alex became 1A, for Amy 1B and for Arthur 1C. Within a short period of time each child knew her/his address and it was decided that whenever a teacher had a note to mail to a child, it needed to have the correct address on it. When a child had a picture for a classmate friend, a letter for a teacher, it was necessary that it be correctly addressed. Being a "mail carrier" became a favorite class job it required sorting and putting the items into the correct boxes.

It was not until I had read Pinocchio and his father sold his own coat to buy a dictionary was an interest in dictionaries sparked. When asked what a dictionary was no one responded. Our room was silent until Alex said, "I think it's a book about words." "It shows what words mean." From this discussion we explored a beginning understanding of dictionaries, which was followed by my searching for a dictionary with one picture, one word on a page. The simplest marketed ones were confusing, so we needed to create our very own, one filled with words that came from stories read aloud. In no time at all we had collected our first ten words—a short word such as "try" to a longer word such as "absolutely". Many of the words children wanted to know were impossible to illustrate, but an attempt was made to have a word and picture for each entry on each page. By the end of the year, our dictionary held forty pages of amazing words which, of course, had to be alphabetized and children attempted to use them in their correct context whenever possible. "Actually" was a favorite, as was "curiosity."

We continued our dictionaries as children went through the alphabet creating multiple words beginning with each letter. Some letters were difficult. What could possibly begin with "Q"? Marcy, a four and a half year old said, "I know—'quit it.' That's a "Q" word." Every child became engaged with words in many different contexts.

Towards the end of the school year children randomly were assigned a letter of the alphabet and asked to bring a snack beginning with their letter. For twenty-six days unusual foods were eaten. Each family was requested to send just enough for a taste of the selected "letter" snack. It was difficult to find foods that began with the letters, "U" and "X", but we teachers had our favorites for those letters, so we provided snacks on those days. "Ugly fruit" was a winner and so was *X-tra* chewing gum. Children brought Celery, Grapes, Marshmallows, Pickles, and many other unusual, sometimes strange foods chosen by children with adult help. Each day, the child responsible for the letter, printed the letter and drew a picture of the food on a card that we then hung on a raised clothesline hung across the room. We had great pictures to look at—pictures from APRICOTS all the way through to ZUCCHINI slices. And so, our class literally digested the alphabet.

The exposure to letters, all the rhymes we made, may have been factors that led to Lisa's story. She was a curly-headed four year old who often had a book in her hands as she "read" a story out loud. Sometimes she could be found under a table, stretched out on her tummy telling a complex tale to another child or two, or talking aloud about a story to herself. Lisa always offered creative ideas for dramatic play, she was a great artist who enjoyed working with clay, paints, using markers, pens and pencils, building puzzles and game playing, but storytelling was what she did best.

One day, while seated on the floor surrounded by four children listening to the imaginative tale she was "reading," holding the book in a way that her audience could see the pictures, she hesitated with her story. She turned a page slowly; she stopped at the word "fry" and turned to me to ask what it said. I thought she paid only a little attention to my response, as she continued her storytelling. When she came across the word "try" she quickly pronounced it. Then in a different voice, not the quiet one of the storyteller she shouted, "Oh my God, I'm reading." That very evening I phoned her home to share the excitement of the day with her parents who were, of course, thrilled.

In each group I taught there were little children who were not ready to print the letters in their names, or recognize their printed name, making parents and children anxious. Once I recognized the stress this created, I required homework for everyone. (Children with older siblings were thrilled; others were unsure what homework meant.) On a Monday I sent the following notes, pinned to each child's back that read:

> Please talk with your child about the age she spoke her first words, and at what age your child began to walk. Send this information back by the end of the week. (Busy parents might need time to have this conversation with their youngster.)

Amazing results! Not every child spoke or walked at the same age—they did so when they were ready. Not every child in school will read and write at the same time. BUT every nursery school child is able to talk and to walk now. So it will be with writing and reading. Given time each child will read and write when he/she is ready. This homework worked wonders for children and their families: the pressure was off.

Over the years my Nursery and Kindergarten classes partnered with second graders who came to our room once a week to read a favorite book with a little non-reading friend. The buzz of the reading, the comments and questions was wonderful. Each second the hen's body—it takes a male and a female to have a chick embryo develop. I found many opportunities to put some sex education into the world of little children—how special for each little boy to recognize the essential role of males in creating life where most of the books talk about the hen sitting on her eggs without a mention of the rooster's role.

Egg hatching was scheduled to begin on the twenty-first day and then each tiny chick, using a special little tooth on its beak, the pippin tooth, was to begin pecking through the membrane and the shell. Children pretended to have such a tooth and nodded and pecked with their heads but could only keep it up for a minute or less when the chicks would work much longer to make the hole through the shell that would allow them to hatch.

Our chicks were right on schedule and children watched the movement from inside of each egg—it took most of the morning giving everyone a chance to look and then go off to build or read or paint or whatever. When tiny, wet little chicks finally completed their arduous job of hatching they needed to rest. Their feathers grader captivated a little listener. Usually the readers came to our room, but occasionally we went to the second grade classroom. We teachers from both classes walked among the readers and listeners to help when it seemed a bit of encouragement might be required. For these fairly new readers, this was a great experience, and for my children, it was very special to have a bigger, older friend share interesting books.

I only repeated some experiences year after year and the following story was one I retold to class after class, to student teachers, to colleagues, to other educators when giving a workshop at conferences because of its superb message. I wanted children to make its message one of their own.

A student's Mother, Dr. O., shared her Nigerian story with my Nursery/Kindergarten children. With children grouped on our rug, situated on a low chair making eye contact as she spoke, Dr. O. held out one hand with her fingers outstretched, and pointing to each finger, so began her story:

> A mother had five children (Dr. O. pointed to her five fingers), and gathering them around her said that she had to leave home to help a neighbor and that the children were to stay home until she returned.

> They all agreed, but as soon she left the first child (Dr. O. pointed to her little pinky finger) said, "I can just go down the road to see if the apples on the tree are ripe. I'll be back before Mother returns, and she'll never know."

> The second child (Dr. O. pointed to her ring finger) said, "I smelled cookies baking at our neighbor's house. I'll run over and get a few, don't tell Mother."

> The third child (Dr. O. pointed to her middle finger) said, "My friend has a new bicycle, and if I go to her

house I know she'll let me try it out and then I'll hurry
back right away."

The fourth child (Dr. O. pointed to her index finger)
said, "I left my skates somewhere and I'm going to look
for them, I'll be back quick as a wink."

Then Dr. O. extended her thumb, pointed to it and said,
"I stand by myself and I think for myself, and what you
say is wrong. I am going to stay here and wait for Mother
to return"

Dr. O. remained quiet for a moment and to the listening children
said: "All through your lives people will tell you to do things, but
if you don't think they are right, hold out your hand, look at your
thumb and do as the story says—STAND BY YOURSELF AND
THINK FOR YOURSELF."

I would, each year, pick a relevant time and place to tell this
story; an important learning tool. On many occasions I would hear
a child, facing another usually with hands on hips say, "If you don't
listen to me, Mrs. Needlman will tell that story again."

Youngsters Dig Archaeology

Since those early days I've had many teaching moments, as well as teaching experiences I want to share. I've tried to capture some insights, learning successes, even failures that deserve to be remembered. In putting my stories on paper I recount the how and why I facilitated and created ways to have learning through play take place for the hundreds of youngsters who were my students. Most of these students, the little children who walked into my classroom five days a week year after year, hated having to miss school on Saturdays and Sundays which made me know I was on the right track as a teacher. Teaching was my passion.

Of the many things that took place, this one, an Archeological Dig, grew from a need to help one particular child; and my whole class enjoyed and learned from it.

Soon after those first weeks of settling into a new school year the days were busy, involved, and comfortable for most of the children. I took special notice of Phyllis, a little five-year old who never spoke or interacted with any of her classmates. She physically separated herself from the others. Over many days of my observing her at different times each day, I saw no changes.

In order to learn more about her to help make her time in school a good experience, I made an appointment to meet with her parents. They told me she was talkative at home with her brother and friends, a cheerful little girl. Their description was so unlike the quiet, withdrawn child I saw each day in my class. It was clear to me we needed to find some way to help Phyllis invest in school. When her mother and father shared their professional involvement with Middle Eastern Studies–both were researchers and professors at the Oriental Institute (henceforth, the OI) at the University–I learned Phyllis spent many hours with them at the OI and yearly accompanied them on digs. It sparked an idea. I asked if perhaps Phyllis showed the class around their workplace, it would give her an opportunity to become involved with classmates. Without hesitating a moment, they invited me to bring the children to not just visit the OI, but to visit the working area in the basement, an area not open to the public. What an opportunity!

I hoped to make it possible for Phyllis to utilize her expertise, share her parents' professional lives and be our guide and "expert" when our class explored this extraordinary Museum. (The OI is situated just two blocks from Lab, a nice walk for us) I planned for our trip.

Once there, Phyllis pointed to different dioramas she really liked because, "I've even been there." (She was born and had visited those faraway places for months at a time each of her five years). "It's really hard work that archeologists do—the sun is hotter than in Chicago and when people dig they get dirty and sweaty". She had words, sometimes even speeches about almost everything we saw. "All of the pots have to be put together like puzzle pieces, and sometimes big chunks are missing. Even my Mom, who knows so much, doesn't always recognize the dug up pieces. They're called shards, and she and my daddy have to do lots of reading before they write stuff down." Kids became interested, some questions were asked but mostly everyone paid attention to Phyllis and to her words and explanations. This was a wonderful visit, and it was just a beginning for all of us.

Phyllis's mother, Professor W, offered help as I began to explore how children might become involved in a "dig" maybe somewhere on campus. My goal was to have Phyllis interested in whatever project we came up with, and be our "expert." The whole idea of a dig, a challenge, was one that I dearly loved.

The exciting part began after I'd made five non-productive calls to the University Department of Building and Grounds (as suggested by Phyllis's father). On my sixth try I found someone who was able to locate the name and then the drawings of the building that had stood on the corner of 58th Street and Woodlawn Avenue. The Buildings & Grounds person identified it as the Gilkey House. I knew of its existence because I had grown up in Hyde Park and as a kid pedaling my bike around the campus I'd seen a large white house with a porch that stood where now there was just a grassy area directly east of the Oriental Institute and diagonally across from the famous Frank Lloyd Wright Robie House.

When I explained to the person on the phone that I was a Nursery/Kindergarten teacher at the Lab Schools, and wanted permission for my children to conduct a dig on that site, my Sherlock Holmes investigative work paid off. I waited several days, and through the interoffice mail I received a copy of the drawing of the actual site, and permission for us to go ahead and dig. At the top of the drawing was a hand written note that said, "COPY OF OLD (1929) SURVEY OF PLAT SHOWING HOUSE LOCATION AT 58TH & WOODLAWN (SW CORNER) GOOD LUCK ON THE DIGS-"

To begin this long-term experience I wanted children to be introduced to what was involved in a dig. I chose to stir up interest by prominently displaying books with photographs and drawings available from our school library. These books brought forth many questions. Each one I'd chosen about the working of archeologists and paleontologists needed to be simplified, (I found no books on the subject written for four and five year olds listeners) but the pictures were worth more than the words. With them as introductory background I was off and running and children were ready for their first "Dig" site, which I planned would take place in our classroom sand table.

One afternoon, when the children were gone, I buried pieces of broken clay flower pots, an old bent spoon, along with several small plastic animals in the sand table, a 6' x 7' open box on legs. Once I'd hidden these items and attached a simple string grid across the table's edge, I drew a copy of this grid on sheets of paper. The site was ready.

I had done my research by visiting an extraordinary dig at the Spertus Museum where I learned how this museum involved children in their mound they referred to as "the tell." My husband made four simple screens for sifting—a necessary part of this involvement. I located little shovels just right for digging.

When all was ready I gathered children around our sand table and explained that at this archeological "dig" each group of four children who signed up on a list would work at one time. When they had questions, Phyllis was the person to answer them. As a buried object was discovered, the "archeologist" was, if possible, to identify it and explain how it could have been used, and then mark on the paper grid where it had been buried. Groups of four took turns digging and sifting the sand, placing marks on the paper grids, reburying the objects while Phyllis was more and more involved. Once every child who was interested had worked at the "site" (this took several school days), they were ready to move on to the next dig site.

Preparation for this phase required communicating with other teachers whose classes shared the playground to gain permission for our taking over the large octagon sand box. We needed two days set aside for just my archeologists to have access for our "dig." Teachers were well acquainted with sharing, and so they agreed. After school hours, when the playground was empty, I buried several pieces of broken dishes, cups and a few other objects that would be of interest to uncover. I then stretched strings across the edges of the box creating a large grid.

On our work days my kids helped place our sign on the box that read:

> **SAND BOX IS ONLY FOR ROOM 110 CHILDREN TUESDAY AND WEDNESDAY MORNINGS THIS WEEK**

The adults read the sign aloud to the children who gathered and the children respected it.

There were many wonderful conversations about the buried treasures, the sifting screens and the strings. Children who were watching joined in with excited screams when an object was unburied and then reburied for the next "archeologists" to locate. Most of the children took a turn digging an area, marking the location of their finds on the new paper grid, but, as expected, there were some children who were uninterested and went off to ride a tricycle or climb and play in another part of the playground. (Not every experience or lesson grabs every child, but that was okay with me.)

Thomas, a serious five year old, asked me to get more books, which I did, and he pored through them looking at the pictures, and asking questions, e.g., "Why are they digging on that hill? "How do they get water? See the bones look wet." Phyllis gave Thomas some satisfying answers and he then offered this information—"My Daddy says being a 'PALEARCHOLOGY' person is a job grownups learn to do when they are in college and that's what I'm going to do." It was Tommy who started some really great conversations with Phyllis and who asked if we could have a real dig, not just one in our room and in the playground.

Here was my opening. I brought out the photocopy of the Gilkey site, and explained that we had permission to begin our real dig near the Oriental Institute where children might find pieces of things buried long ago. The size of our site had to be smaller than those Tommy found in our books. Ideas for it were talked about, and finally it was agreed to mark off a space one meter on all four sides that would be a square a child said, and then dig one meter down. Phyllis happily agreed to help since she knew about digs. The kids were more than ready to begin a weekly Tuesday journey to the place shown on the paper where the house once stood.

For our first Tuesday morning children helped to pack a meter stick, all the short-handled yard shovels we could borrow, chunks of chalk for marking the dig space, a plastic cloth, (an old shower curtain from my house) our sifting screens and small spades which we squeezed into the wagon. I carried a square plywood board for covering the dig hole. This unusual procession was made of children who took turns pushing and/or pulling the load across two streets to our site.

The day was a bright sunny one and children eagerly unloaded the wagon, measured and chalk-marked a one meter square before taking up the shovels to begin the work. It took many of us, kids, and adults (Phyllis's parents along with my teaching assistants) working to remove the grass. These chunks of soil and grass were then dumped onto the plastic cloth. The one meter depth planned for was not reached (a good thing because it would have been easy for some children to jump down, but getting out could have been a real problem.)

Tommy, as expected along with Martin, Sarah, and Carol were the first to measure and then dig. A few others sifted the extracted dirt from the hole, while Molly, Ben and several others preferred to play on the adjacent grassy space seemingly uninterested in the "work." Each shovel dumped on the plastic contained dirt, stones, and occasionally some worms, (Ah, food for our toad back in our classroom). One or two shovels of dirt held recognizable objects—a piece identified as a bone possibly left from someone's dinner, and a chunk of pottery from a dish. Each shovel of dirt was sifted and the diggers separated the good stuff from the parts that went onto the plastic. The time spent with involved children was a little less than an hour on this first real dig experience, but before we headed back with the wagon filled with tools, worms and "artifacts," the hole had to be covered with the plywood board for safety purposes. I'd written on it:

> **PLEASE DO NOT DISTURB—
> EXCAVATION SITE**

The plastic cloth, now piled with dirt, remained at the site alongside the printed board. Back in our classroom we talked about what had taken place, what had been accomplished, and Phyllis, now well into being our Dig Expert, made suggestions for our next Tuesday's work. "Everyone needs to wear gloves, on REAL digs that's what they do, and everyone needs to be more careful pulling the wagon with the "finds" back to the room—maybe we should put the worms in a bucket with some dirt." (Being in charge, the new role for Phyllis was working.)

I explained the plan we'd follow was gathering the needed supplies, remembering to bring along a bucket for worms, packing gloves and loading our wagon every Tuesday for the "Dig."

On the second Tuesday's trip we found the board covering the site had been re-written by some people from the Oriental Institute (most likely Phyllis' parents) and it now read:

PRE ARCHAELOGOGY I
EXCAVATION SITE
BEGUN APRIL 25, 1995
UNIVERSITY OF CHICAGO
LAB SCHOOL
KINDERGARTEN/
NURSERY CLASS
N.W. CORNER FOUNDATION:
GILKEY HOUSE
SITE SUPERVISOR:
G. NEEDLMAN

As our "dig" site was situated diagonally across from Robie House, each Tuesday children were digging, busloads of curious Frank Lloyd Wright's visitors crossed the street to read our sign which we had propped against a tree, and to watch children dig, sift and screech with excitement when any artifacts or worms were discovered. Visitors were very interested, and asked "How old are you? What are you doing? What will you do with the things you dig up?" They seemed delighted to hear that the children were being "Archeologists". Phyllis spoke up answering most of their questions. (If you know the picture book, *Mike Mulligan and His Steam Shovel,* you'll recognize children responded in much the way Mike in the story did—the more people watched the faster and better they dug.)

In a reply to my thanking the OI folks for the great words on our board, they sent an important email saying it was their expectation that half of our dig findings be shared with the Oriental Institute. Children agreed, theirs was a fair request. We offered some of our worms.

Over our digging trips, shards of dishes, bent metal spoons and forks, things that may have been dried egg shells, along with some unidentifiable objects were found by the sifting "Archeologists." These finds, now named artifacts, were brought to our classroom after being carefully carried in the wagon, were brushed and or washed ready to become an exhibit for our class room Archeological Museum.

Children found that to dig almost one cubic meter took time and hard work and created what appeared to be an enormous dirt pile on the old shower curtain cloth. These paleontologists worked six Tuesdays and fortunately, on each of these days the weather was clear and dry. On the last day as they began to fill the hole by shoveling the soil from the plastic ready to jump and flatten it, it began to drizzle. The dirt filled the excavation site. To everyone's surprise, buried underneath the pile that had been mounded on the plastic, children found dried pieces of grass sod that had been removed on day one. Kids placed the little bits of dried grass on top of the piled dirt, and the rains gently fell watering the site making the space look almost untouched.

Children created signs written in inventive spelling. "A *Spon"* (a spoon). *"Dnr Bon"* (dinner bone). *"1 pce of a dsh"* (one piece of a dish). The labeled objects were placed on a table that had been covered in black paper so the "artifacts" looked important. This table became the Classroom Museum. My Archeologists wrote invitations for other classes to come visit the Museum. As invited guests arrived, Phyllis described our "Dig" while other children talked about the sand table and the play-yard digs that took place earlier.

Phyllis was, during and following out "Dig," well set as a functioning part of the classroom, and for the remainder of the year she engaged with one or more of the kids during the day, chose to sit next to friends at lunch, and entered the classroom eager to have her school day start.

Mission accomplished!

That grassy area we once worked on no longer exists. In its place University landscapers put lovely benches, beautiful flower beds, and winding pathways. Many years later, Benjy, grown up, recalled the experience, and over coffee in my kitchen fondly talked about our "Dig."

I wasn't able to locate the books I brought into the classroom but found instead titles of three books each with wonderful pictures of "digs" worth locating, should you want to have such a great experience with young children.

Art & Archeology, by Shirley Glubok, 1966.

Digging to the Past, Excavations in Ancient Lands, by John Hackwell, 1986.

The Illustrated Atlas of Archaeology. Warwick Press, 1982

Numbers Make Cents

And my stories continue. I was told by many children they could count to 100 or to 500 or beyond, but I found the counting exhibited rote repetition that seldom was meaningful. I aimed to change that. Numbers became part and parcel of each day as they were encountered in meaningful places beyond our Dig and our mailboxes.

Children often drove or raced small cars along the floor, which led me to measuring eleven spaces on a line, numbering 0–10 and covering it in clear tape. With no predetermined idea of how it would be used, I was certain somehow, some child would incorporate it into meaningful play, and perhaps some learning would grow from it.

Donny noticed it and slowly drove his truck from one end of the line to the other calling out 1, 3, 2,"oh"; the only numbers this three and a half year old recognized. After all "o" was part of his name, and zero wasn't yet in his vocabulary. Children soon queued up seemingly with a purpose in mind—Jennifer walked a small doll house lady from number to number, while other children made cars, or trucks rumble along the line. For weeks it was actively used. Some children identified the numbers out loud as it was walked or driven over and I loved hearing, "That's 4 like I am."

Marcy started at ten and counted backwards and blasted her car off while other children cheered her on, and then followed her example. This taped line was put to many good uses.

I left the numbers unchanged for several weeks, and when I noted its use had dwindled and it was still well fastened, I added a piece of the same tape and extended the numbers to 20. Kids love challenges and fresh materials, and this longer number line was just that. Some days it was completely ignored, and for reasons I could never figure out, it sometimes invited new play and exposure. When a tiny stop sign appeared next to the numbers or some other addition or change was made, children found different ways to incorporate numbers in their "work". Numbers appeared on easel drawings and on signs affixed to block structures and walls–not always drawn correctly, but close enough for recognition. Inventive printing was very acceptable and encouraged. No, I didn't extend the line further because our rug areas and furniture blocked the way, and I didn't want to move the line into the hallway. For its lifetime it remained a zero to twenty line.

Part of our daily routine was for children to keep track of the number of days they were in school. The count began with Zero which indicated there were days that happened before school began. These numbers, written on small adhesive-backed cards were placed at eye level around the entire room with each tenth number drawn with a different color marker. We made a big deal and popped corn to celebrate the tenth, twentieth, thirtieth days, etc. and everyone had a cup of popcorn and sometimes un- popped corn kernels. Part of the fun involved counting out the corn in groups of ten before being eaten. The sounds of the popping, the counting, and the giggling were great.

The hundredth day of school was a Very Special one. It wasn't only celebrated in my room but in each of the early childhood classrooms at Lab School—a part of a math program we all followed, each teacher having a slightly different interpretation of it. Starting a week in advance while the daily counting was in the 90s, I'd send notes home asking families to pull together 100 items of whatever they wanted that would fit in 8 oz. cup. On the 100th day, children brought cups of paper clips, bottle caps, chocolate chips, tooth picks tied into packs of 10, straws, a stringed necklace made out of 100 oat cereals along with other creative collections. These cups were arranged on a table for everyone to see, count, touch. Some of the items such as the hundred screws were returned but only after they had been counted. We made use of the hundred paint swatches in the art area, and of course, the candy was eaten.

I often would say, "Think of a number that is bigger than six, but smaller than eight. What is it?" Problems like this were asked whenever children were in line waiting to go outside, to the library or at dismissal time, the transition times. Once simple number questions were comfortably answered I made them more challenging. "Tell me the numbers that are less than 10 but more than 6." Numbers were exciting and children were delighted to be involved learning about them. I must admit, many of the minute number games came from an existing Math program, and many of them were simply improvised ideas that I take full credit for creating.

Even music played a part in number recognitions. We fortunately had an old, but in-tune piano that attracted most children. When I realized fists and sometimes objects were being used to bang on the keys, I called a meeting to figure out how to best care for this musical instrument. I made sure to steer our conversation until it was decided only fingers were to make music. All of the big decisions made included children's involvement. I am sure we held a worthwhile discussion about the piano though the particulars are now lost in time.

I had removed the front panel of our upright piano so the hammers, attached to each of the keys, were exposed and small clusters of kids watched what happened when "musicians" pressed keys—the hammers hit the strings. There was a need to put up two signs; one to remind the musicians—HANDS ONLY ON KEYS, and another, EYES ONLY for the hammers. These simple pictures signs acted as constant reminders and kept me from nagging. (I worked at having any rules, whenever possible, tell children what to do, and refrained from the "No" rules too often used.)

With my trusty permanent marker, I carefully numbered an octave of piano keys beginning with middle C–ONE through EIGHT. I remember Amy asked what the numbers were all about. Rather than answer, I handed her two pieces of music made on lined music paper with the words of familiar simple songs. Under each word I had a number that corresponded to those found on the keys, 1,1,4,4,5,5,4. Amy looked at the numbers, and then pressed the corresponding keys—a great pause between each one, and finally she said "It plays Twinkle, Twinkle and I made it do that." Of course, one song wasn't sufficient, so I created more sheets of music—words and numbers. Looking up at the numbers and down at the keys was difficult for most of the children, but there were those who mastered it while on lookers watched the hammers hitting the strings and some clapped or sang along. How special to have use of the piano by children and not just by adults.

We were fortunate to have a pet toad children named; my granddaughter had found it in her Cleveland yard. We never knew its sex–he or maybe she was a delightful animal for our classroom. It was special in that Cleveland introduced addition and subtraction to youngsters to mention just one of its attributes. Cleveland ate anything that moved, and when we ran out of live food for it I'd place dried flies (purchased from a pet shop) into a plastic bowl along with Cleveland and gently tap the bottom of the bowl making whatever was there move about. If toad had used up the dried flies supplies, little pieces of left over lunch scraps ended up being jiggled in the bowl and then consumed. Since both Toad and the "food" at these feeding times were in an enclosed container, only a few children were able to observe the eating. The solution was to have the children seated on the perimeter of our rug with a large sheet of white paper in the center which made a great feeding place for Cleveland. Most days children were able to dig up insects from our play yard. But in the winter they had to dig next to the building walls in the court yard, under the decaying leaves to find millipedes, worms or strange bugs which than became treats for Cleveland and also a math lesson. There were the days I captured and maimed a roach or two so they were still able to move. (We did have them in our old building.) Children counted each critter on the paper before Toad was gently placed in the midst of them. He/she moved from one to another and in seconds, if we had four insects moving, Cleveland would grab one and everyone knew, without ever recounting, there were three left. Should he/she then gobble two more, children called out, "One left" Toad had four and five year old children counting, adding and subtracting making learning fun and playful.

Occasionally a child from a nearby classroom would burst into our room to ask if Toad could come to a locker where there were ants. Children would rush into the hallway to see and try to count, but many ants moved too quickly and counting wasn't possible. I timed Toad and in a few seconds it had all the ants eaten from the floor of the locker where food had fallen. Cleveland must have loved these treats – he/she never left even a tiny ant alive. What a great vacuum cleaner and teacher our amphibian pet proved to be.

Becky confided in me that when she told her big sister what Toad does, "Eats live bugs," her sister said that was gross, but Becky's response was, "No it is Nature."

My Kindergarten/Nursery class room was located on the first floor of the large three-story Laboratory School building. Lunch milk cartons were delivered to the second floor (something I never did understand) the Principal's office and library were also upstairs as was the closet that held our paper supplies and the laminating machine. At one time or another each of my students had a reason to walk to the second floor alone or with the group, but the only learning experience this created was to recognize "right" from "left." To be safe, children were expected to hold onto the railing using their right hand. (I made a point of explaining on streets and roads in our country, all vehicles must stay on the right side, and when people cross streets they must look both ways and especially to the right to cross safely). Each child knew to hold on to the railing with his/her right hand going up the stairs, but questioned how it could be used when going down. Much to their amazement, their right hands were still used, they did not change. Once it was experienced over and over with each trip up the stairs and down, it was understood that even turned around right hands were unchanged. (And experiencing meant to notice repeatedly the place of their right hand. For some children it meant having a washable marker and drawing of a happy face on the right hand, or putting a colored piece of tape on one finger on the right hand.) This was good, but I thought of something else to make walking up and down the staircase more of a learning experience. There were times, especially on rainy days that we walked beyond the second up to the third floor just for the fun of exploring, and to get some exercise.

I scrounged the neighborhood Recycling Center and located a stack of bold, black two inch square numbers – a pile of many zeroes through nines. Having found them set this project in motion. I invited volunteers from my class to accompany me to number the stairs from the first to the second floor To do this job we'd need a bucket of water, a few used sponges, (No need to use new ones for this dirty job) some rags for drying, a roll of heavy clear tape and those found numbers. More than a few hands were raised of children wanting to be volunteers, and I explained that everyone would be able to help as all of the stairs were to be numbered from the first to the second floor. Later children voted to extend numbering up to the third floor.

These first volunteers were eager to do anything that seemed out of the ordinary, and my classroom always had projects that fit that description. I knew they didn't fully understand what they would be doing but they were ready to get to work. I explained their first job was to scrub clean and then dry the corner of teach stair so the number and the tape we'd use to cover and protect it could stick and stay in place even with all the feet that travelled the stairs. (Even at the Lab School, housekeeping doesn't get into corners) The far back right corner on each step was to have its proper number, but kids had to tell me what number belonged on the floor before the first stair. As expected, I was told. "Start with ONE" but then Chloe, my tiniest Nursery School child whose older brother was a math whiz, a second grader, reminded the group we started our number line at zero and her brother always said there were numbers that were called minus or negative ones and they came before ONE." We have to start the stairs with ZERO."

The children agreed with Chloe, and ZERO was placed in the corner on the floor followed by 1, 2, on the steps. Each of the three workers repeated washing and drying, selecting the next consecutive number from the pile and covering it with tape. There were fourteen stairs up to the landing, followed by another fourteen, so it took many days and many working crews to number each stair. Along the way, while it was "a work in progress" I would hear children counting aloud and asking whoever was near, "When will the other stairs have their own numbers?"

Once the job was completed, those children with long enough legs walked taking in stride two stairs at a time and counting out loud by 2's. My little children soon figured out how to count by twos. A few much bigger kids took three steps at a time, so even more learning took place. Counting backwards was easy. Most children those days, back in the 70's and 80's knew to blast off and they called out ten, nine, eight, seven, six, five, four, three, two one,--blast off, and that is what was most often heard while coming from the second to the first floor.

Of course wear and tear on any well used place requires maintenance and old numbers needed to be removed, the floor space scrubbed and new numbers put in their places. Year after year this became a task I did with different groups of children in my class. (Long after I retired but still returned to borrow books from the second floor library or make a visit to the office, our numbers were still in place. Some other teacher had recognized the learning that took place with this simple application, and took time and effort to keep it up.)

In the fall of 2013 Lab expanded and a brand new Earl Shapiro Early Childhood Center was opened. I don't see any signs that indicate those stairs will be numbered.

Seems to me not all progress is completely positive.

Patterning and More

Some days at rug time children literally became pattern pieces. I'd invite a selected group of children to stand next to each other. A good example would be the day I called four children with long hair and four children with short hair to stand. I then arranged them in a line of longhair-shorthair, longhair-shorthair, longhair- shorthair, longhair- shorthair. As they stood I selected two of the seated children to stand and become part of this pattern. Those newly selected children had to recognize the pattern and fit into themselves into it. Once everyone seemed to "catch on" patterning changed. I might choose children because of the color of their clothing, or shoes with ties, or shoes with fasteners, shirts with collars, shirts without collars—no end of choices. I seldom if ever could stump the children once they recognized what the pattern was all about. Given enough exposure, they suggested and created their own patterns and everyone was required to figure out if a pattern was chosen because of sock color, the number of buttons on their shirts, or was the choice of new shoes, old shoes, and on and on. From each pattern group, one seated child was certain to figure it out and explain it to the rest of the children. I always encouraged the child who guessed to select someone who hadn't had a turn that day. It was playful, engaging and that is what a rug time needed to be.

I made pattern cards with pictures of shapes— circle, triangle, square, circle, triangle, square, circle, triangle, square, or square, circle, circle, square, circle, circle were created. The idea was to have different arrangements making up the patterns. These cards, laminated to assure them a long life, were stored in the bins along with the small shape blocks that matched the pictures. There were simple card patterns along with more complicated ones, and children chose to work with them during their free choice times. Here was my way to reinforce pattern skills, and by making it available children had opportunities to engage in the activity on their own. These cards were well used over time.

In the art area children made small clay balls which, when air dried, became beads as soon as a hole was pierced through them. Pattern cards were drawn and followed to make necklaces: e.g., one clay bead, one button, one bead, one button, or the pattern was two clay beads, one button, two clay beads, one button, or even more complicated pattern of one clay bead, one button, two clay beads, one button, one clay beads, two buttons, (1-1-1-2-1-2-1-2). Some children created fairly complicated patterns, and children made bead necklaces which were sold at a Parent Fundraiser event. They were purchased much to the joy of their creative math designers.

Making bead necklaces.

Often books we shared led to meaningful projects and Rolf Myller's book *How Big is a Foot?* inspired yet another math involvement. Ah, numbers and how they were woven into many parts of the classroom environment.

I asked if any family could lend us a shoe that measured 12 inches, and lo and behold, one was actually found—a man's shoe exactly one foot long. Once it was in my possession I put my own family to work. My husband, our three children and I spent an evening using colored construction paper tracing and cutting out one foot long shoes along with many one inch colorful paper squares.

To begin this activity required parent helpers, since knowing the height of each of the twenty-four children was needed. The most accurate way, and the one that was most fun was to have a child lay on the floor with her/his head touching a wall, so an adult could measure and record the number of feet, the number of inches onto a card. There were so many ways to obtain this measurement, but adults and children preferred this one. When there was a record for each child, and this took many days, and many parent helpers, a child then went to the art table, found the card with her/his name, selected the number and colors of the feet and inches, her/his height, and pasted them on a long narrow sheet of paper. Once each child's name and the needed number of cut-out feet (usually three) and the required number of inch squares (some as many as seven) were in place, these measurement papers were hung around the room.

They were admired, compared, and the feet and inches counted numerous times before they were rolled up and sent home. I much later learned many families kept them for a long time. Sorry to say I don't know if any still exist.

Some mornings a hurried parent would ask if there was a cracker I could give her child as there was "No time for breakfast at home" or a child, upon entering the room, asked when would snacks be ready? It didn't take too many of these comments to realize that some children entered the classroom not having had time for any breakfast, let alone an adequate one. (Fortunately I had access to a list from the school nurse of children with food allergies at the start of the school year.) My solution for making food available those mornings was to create a "restaurant table," *MacNeedlman's*, and it would be opened for customers. Some mornings it accommodated as many as six children, but most days there were only three or four youngsters checking the menu, and sitting down. Whenever possible the menu was "written" by children in the art area, usually appearing in some fashion of print, creatively spelled and, of course, illustrated. On any day the choices might be juice, warmed milk with graham crackers, dry cereals and milk, or crackers and cheese depending on what was available from my food shelf or in the small classroom refrigerator.

Children ate, chatted, then cleared their places and were off to activities of their choosing or to our morning meeting. Before leaving the "restaurant" they were expected to figure the cost of their meal—all items were 2 or 3 cents and children learned to add the numbers and every once in a while a child would include an extra penny and say 'it's a tip." No coins were exchanged instead the amount was tapped on the table or in an adult's hand, counting aloud as the charge was being tapped.

Much the way a coffeehouse functions, our breakfast café served its patrons well. Having a comfortable tummy made the day a positive one.

Children experienced more involvements with numbers and again, food played a role. When lunches were finished, we all ate together at tables in our classroom, children with freshly washed index fingers waited their turn to buy a "Needlman Special." I either smeared each extended finger with peanut butter, or if a child was allergic, cream cheese worked, and dipped the sticky finger with whatever crumbs were left in the container from snack time. Sometimes I coated crushed graham crackers, sometimes bits of vanilla wafers, or even cereals. My "Specials" changed daily. Here's where the math came into play. The way I was paid—and the price changed depending on the crumbs—was for a child to tap the palm of my hand a number of times that represented the price, same as at the restaurant for breakfasts. I would take payment in pennies from Nursery School children, but Kindergarteners were expected to pay with pretend nickels or dimes and depending on the price of my "Special." I had to be told what change was to be received. The price one day might have been three cents, so I received three taps from the Nursery School shoppers, and a nickel from a Kindergartener who wanted two taps change. Since the lines were always long, those children waiting their turn overheard the money exchange and soon the Nursery School children were able to tell me if a "Special" cost six cents, and a child gave me a dime, I was to give four cents, four taps, in change. We did amazing math each day, and no one ever tired of purchasing a "Special" and figuring out the cost. (Lunch specials required many jars of peanut butter and cream cheese that I shopped for when purchasing my family groceries. It was hardly unique that I spent my own money on needed items—it's what teachers do.)

Since not all children became hungry at the same time, mid-morning snacks were made available to accommodate each child's time clock. Two children, the servers, had the job of setting up snacks for the table which was open for an hour of each morning. A child could, if there was an empty seat, help her/himself, sit and chat with friends, clear the space, put her/his used cup in a bin with soapy water—we had a double sink in the room and an adult used a hot water rinse before hanging the cups back on the cup rack ready for the next child. Time was that we used only paper cups, but changed when environmental issues could be talked about and paper cups were replaced by colorful plastic ones, carefully washed and used over and over. We saved paper and trees, and kept the paper cups out of landfill. My husband built a delightful cup stand—the height allowed even the shortest child to reach the top to take off or hang up a cup.

Each morning's snack consisted of water or juice served in several small pitchers, comfortable for small hands to pour successfully. They were placed on the table along with either bowls of crackers, dry cereals, fresh fruits, or veggies, sometimes cheese squares. Alongside the bowls I'd place appropriate signage cards that had pictures of 2 and 2 more crackers, or 1 plus 1 plus 1, or 3 and 1. Each day there were different "problems" making it necessary for children to figure out how large, or small a helping was acceptable. Only addition problem cards appeared at first, then subtraction, (five minus 2, or three minus zero) and eventually the cards had a combination of problems but only after each concept seemed to be understood. The cards required that children look carefully to be sure to have the number of snacks for the day. At first the cards were simply drawn pictures of crackers or one or more spoons for small veggies, later numbers took the place of pictures and then formulas—2+3 or 7-5 used, but first every child had to become familiar and confident with the pictures. Even eating provided an experience for children to engage in math, in using numbers in meaningful ways.

Children's Insightful Words

———•———

To share stories that aren't about children's learning, but my learning, I listened to their words which often provided me with some meaningful insights into the workings of their minds. If only I had kept more complete notes of the many incredible words of my preschool and kindergarten kids, but here is hindsight at work once again.

One day, Sam, age 3, while seated on my lap, gently stroked my cheek. He screwed up his little face as he looked at me and asked *"Why do you have all those cracks on your face."* I responded, *"Because I'm getting old."* Then I said, *"No, that's not true, it is because I am old."*

I really do believe honesty is always the best policy.

Another child, who proudly stated she was three and three quarters, told me her Mother said I was good-natured. I paused, smiled and asked what she thought her mother meant by "good-natured" and she replied, *"You know, you're good and you bring worms for Toad."*

On a walk around the campus I stopped to look at some little blooming flowers and named them *Forsythia*. Four year old Sophia quickly said, "Oh no, they are for me."

A child and I were heading upstairs to laminate a photo and my little one asked, "Are we taking this to be eliminated?"

During a resting time the recording I played was by Dvorak and after listening for a few minutes, Karl said, "That's classical. It's like music where people play violins."

A three and a half year old, Sonja was wearing a tee shirt with a picture of Sleeping Beauty on it. I asked her, "Are you Sleeping Beauty?" Her response was, "No, I'm an awake beauty."

While out walking one day a four year old stopped to look at lovely flowers blooming and said, "That blue one is an In Patient and the pink one is an Out Patient." (His parents are doctors)

"I know what weddings are all about. Everybody gets a piece of cake." said by Akemi, age four.

Sarah was involved with a clump of *Play-Doh* while proceeding to pound it with both hands. When asked what she was making she replied, "A Pound Cake of course." (I should have known)

I overheard a comment made on the playground when Sam, a four year old grabbed the shovel Mark (age three) was using. Mark's quick response was to say, "I'm not going to invite you to my Birthday Party." And without missing a beat, Sam said, "Yes you will because by

tomorrow you'll forget all about this." (Mighty good
insight for a four year old)

One morning while everyone was seated on our rug
ready to share a book, Marcy who looked sad said, "My
father was fired." I looked at the faces of the children and
one little boy looked horrified. I suddenly understood
the word FIRED terrified him. I asked if anyone could
explain what Marcy meant by the word "fired." Ideas
and words tumbled forth and together we made it clear
"fired" did not mean being caught in a blaze of a fire.
More children than one looked relieved. Marcy then
changed her statement and said she meant her Daddy's
job had ended and now he wouldn't go to work.

From these and other conversations I came to realize children
may hear our words but find they have different meanings. A nursery
school child summed up many misunderstandings when he said "I
hear your words. I just don't understand what they mean."

(I should have sent notes of thanks to the many children who
sat on my lap over the years and sneezed or coughed in my face, and
in so doing gave me incredible immunity. I do not get colds. I often
wonder how long this immunity will last. So far, so good!)

Not only are words taken at their literal meaning, but written
stories in books are difficult to distinguish between fiction and
nonfiction.

I always read aloud many times throughout each day and I'd
make a point of describing each book as being fiction or non-fiction
using those grown up words. I'd read books on many subjects, birds,
environments, housing, slavery, freedom, loving, to name a few, and
children learned to identify them as non-fiction or fiction. They
were comfortable with the words for made up stories by authors and
stories that came from real facts. Big words, big ideas were special
and were often used in and out of context.

With this as background when I was invited to introduce a children's author at an adult gathering of a group, The Children's Reading Roundtable, I asked my children what they thought I should say about her. One child said, "Just say she is both." I needed an explanation, and my little one said, "You know, her stories are fiction and nonfiction." This author, Joanna Cole, wrote the wonderful *Magic School Bus* series, and actually she was both—a fiction and a nonfiction wonderful story teller. My intro was well received, and Joanna was delighted with the idea that came from the children and their understanding of her writings.

Another example of fiction/nonfiction came from a book that became a favorite: *Miss Nelson is Missing*, by Harry Allard, Jr. In the story children believed that their teacher, Miss Nelson, lived in their classroom. This whimsical tale so delighted my group that I decided we'd take a trip to my home. For that first trip we travelled by bus since at that time I lived a distance from school. Trips in later years—and there were many—were walking ones. However near or far we traveled the purpose was always the same: I thought it fun and important for the children to discover that I was a parent, a wife, a mother and that I really did live in a house, not in the school. Before the trip I'd explain that I only invite friends to my home, and friends understand furniture is for sitting on, and closed doors should stay closed. Once we arrived children explored almost every room in our home. Several went to the upstairs bathroom my own children used with its large mirror on one wall, and as they looked in it, with me standing behind, one little one said, "When you go home you're a Mommy." Wow, they got it!

I had to search for and collect the children who had travelled all over the house to join me in our kitchen for snacks, and then we boarded the bus and headed back to school. Of course, I read the *Miss Nelson* book again and again.

Once we'd moved into the University community we walked to our home. For these trips I made simple maps showing the streets we'd cross, drew the one-way signs and a few outstanding features we'd pass along the way. I explained that our home had a very long hallway meant for running, and children only needed to stay to the right, just like on the school stairs, to keep it safe. (We live on the first floor and no one lives below us so running was okay with me.)

Most years our house visits were unstructured. Before leaving school I talked about my indoor garden with its many plants and a water fountain with a little boy who pees—quite a way to stir up a group. We followed the maps, but once we arrived every child gravitated to the fountain with its statue and proceeded to touch the water and giggle. They counted the metal insects, abandoned nests and painted birds located in and among my plants. Some children moved off to watch the fish swimming in my tank while others waited for a turn to play the one-armed bandit, an antique slot machine that works without requiring nickels and does not pay out. (My husband made it child-friendly years back.)

The trips that seemed to be most meaningful were when I shared my holiday of Passover, a freedom celebration. Children stood around my long table (no room for 23 chairs) as I related a very simplified version of the Passover story that held everyone's attention. The parents who accompanied us on the walk helped serve a few traditional foods—matzos, *charoses* (a delicious mixture of apples, cinnamon, grape juice and nuts—no nut allergies known back then—that represented mortar used when Jews were slaves); and I served white grape juice, knowing that when it was spilled, and that would certainly happen, it wouldn't stain as would the red. Looking for the hidden *Afikomen* is an important part of the tradition and searching for it was exciting. A Seder, the service before the meal, cannot end without the sharing of a small piece of this special *Afikomen* matzo. The children who found it were given a gift of a plant clipping of their choice from my garden.

The visits to my home were popular on many levels. I believed our relationship of teacher/student grew closer when children had opportunities to see me as a person beyond the classroom so we made the journey yearly.

Composting, Chick Hatching, Our Menagerie

Eating lunches involved food scraps children threw in the garbage. This was changed when I introduced composting and began a compost bin. I purchased a suitable box from the neighborhood recycling center, a favorite place to shop, and filled it part way with soil and dried leaves along with several hundred red worms I ordered from a supply company catalogue. Each day, when lunches were finished, two children had the job of collecting any leftover fruit cores and peels, scraps of vegetables, usually carrots, celery or lettuce pieces, to put into our small food processor. These chopped up food bits were then ready to bury in the compost bin, covered with some soil, dead leaves brought from the play yard, or torn newspaper scraps. In no time at all, the special worms (red wigglers) devoured the food bits; they ate that would have become garbage. We added crushed eggshells, other bits and pieces left from our cooking and baking projects, making sure to cover them. The worm castings and their droppings increased. It wasn't long before we had rich soil for a small garden we planted just outside our classroom. More than fifteen years later, when I became a Master Composter through the University of Illinois Extension, I realized we had been composting in my classroom long before it become popular to do so in schools.

In our small garden space adjacent to the classroom, we grew and harvested foods (mostly grasses) that were then fed to the birds living in our aviary, to our guinea pig that loved the fresh green shoots, and our toad that enjoyed an occasional sprout. Other teachers were concerned that the compost box would attract rodents because of the decaying matter, but we kept the scraps covered with dried leaves and/or shredded newspaper and never had a problem. We did not compost shortenings, meats, fish, or bread scraps. Today there are many ways to compost indoors. I loved the book you'll find in the bibliography, *Worms Eat My Garbage*, by Mary Appelhof, a book I discovered long after we composted in my room at Lab.

Jean Piaget, a world famous psychologist and educator's theory on conservation fascinated me. His research was easily demonstrated as children played at our water table. He stated that young children are incapable of understanding quantity, length or number of items unrelated to the arrangement or appearance of the object or items. For me, the proof was in seeing it play out.

I would set up the water table (filled with sand at times and used as our first "Dig" site) for pouring activities making available short fat unbreakable containers, tall thin ones, and an assortment of in-between sizes and shapes for children to use. As they played and poured water from one container to the other I would question which one held the most water? The tallest one always won. When a child emptied one container into another and water from the shorter fatter one overflowed the tall slender one I would again ask again which one holds the most water? Most youngsters stick to their guns, convinced that the tallest one held the most.

Whenever I spaced six books close together and six books separated by a few inches, a young child would tell me there were more books on the line with spaces. Certainly this bit of information, the theory of conservation, fits perfectly into experimenting with numbers—taller is bigger, longer is more. For young children these are facts even though they are not accurate.

My background and child development knowledge helped me provide flexible expectations for the children in my nursery and kindergarten classes. I did keep in mind there are no hard fast rules that every child follows, though I found it important to know what was within reach of a child's age range or whether certain involvements were even possible.

The water table was a place for a variety of water play, and at times for experiments. The play there was often dictated by the items I made available. It became a Laboratory when children found small eyedroppers, plastic test tubes in racks, and bottles of colored water in it. They could put on lab jackets (doctor coats with their sleeves cut to fit little arms, donated from doctor parents who practiced at the University hospital), and go to "work". Many of my students were familiar with laboratories as one or both of their parents were involved in some aspect of the sciences on campus. In the white lined table children discovered how to fill the eyedroppers, moved liquids from one container to another, as they engaged in meaningful and satisfying play. My role in this Laboratory was to ask questions of a working child that required thought to reply. "Why do you think the water in the test tube turned green"? "Tell me what you did to make the color pink." or "How can you change the color of that test tube?"

Some days children played with soapy water in the table, and by introducing different objects to bubble play, i.e. open plastic circles, bent wires, children blew strange shaped bubbles. When a wetted finger touched a bubble, it did not pop—what fun!

At other times I filled a pan with powdered dry cornstarch and several containers of water waiting for a child or children to explore. When these small "scientists" mixed the two ingredients, cornstarch with water, their properties changed. If in motion, which was accomplished by taking a glob of it and rolling it between their hands, the somewhat liquid cornstarch became a solid, however, when left in a still state, just in the bowl, it turned to liquid. The best feature of cornstarch "work" was that once it dried, it easily could be swept off clothing, hands, and even floors. It was messy when wet, but very manageable when dry. Colored water mixed with white cornstarch added to the interest and attracted many children. Even when I refrained from becoming involved, the water table was a wonderful place to overhear the interesting conversations, statements, and/or questions raised by engrossed children. One year I was unsuccessful closing the holes in the bottom of the well-used table liner (duct tape didn't do the job). This was an important piece of equipment so I ordered a new table pan from a catalogue. The company no longer made a white one, instead only a colored plastic insert liner could be ordered. A colored pan limited its use as children could no longer mix yellow and blue water and change it to green—wonderful blending discoveries were no longer possible. To continue our "experimentation with color mixing" it was necessary that I placed a white bowl inside the colored table for children to enjoy vegetable colored water and test tubes.

I sent a letter to the company complaining that what they may have thought was an improvement was really a mistake. Their apology came too late—our room had a red table liner, and unfortunately, they did not offer to send a replacement—a no-win happening.

As expected, in our old building on campus, we had mice problems that existed long before we began composting. Adorable little brown field mice, brazen and bold, made their way into our classroom. They would scurry around as I met with other teachers or parents after hours, or even as children were playing. One day after having read aloud the delightful story, *The Mouse and the Motorcycle*, by Beverly Cleary, I brought half of a ping pong ball, and a little toy motorcycle to our rug time, and on showing the new objects to the children questioned if a mouse in our room was smart enough to put on the helmet and learn to ride as one had in the story. I explained I didn't think we would likely be around to see it, but maybe when it was nighttime and the room was quiet and dark after everyone had gone home, maybe then one would ride. Children checked the motorcycle location daily, but unfortunately, our mouse just wasn't clever enough.

Not only did we have mice but somehow children contacted head lice and this was one of my solutions for making a horrid situation manageable and fun. Head lice posed an enormous problem. Children, parents, the school nurse, all of us, were tired of the time it took to have heads checked before coming into the room each day, and at home to have shampoos, and combings with fine-toothed combs. When it seemed as though everyone was rid of the pests—it took a long time—I thought it would be fun to scratch like monkeys, make "cheee-cheee" sounds, and have children check each other out, monkey style. What was a horror became playful as children, seated on the rug, turned to each other, scratching, making those high pitched sounds, and picking at heads. It was silly and fun to do.

Everyone was familiar with lice eggs unfortunately, but being involved in hatching chicken eggs was a positive experience. My part involved both careful planning and time, but was so meaningful that year after year it was an important piece of the kindergarten curriculum for me and my colleagues.

If you've been to the Museum of Science and Industry in Chicago with young children, you've most likely stopped to watch chicks hatching. Well, the University of Illinois Extension provided free fertilized eggs for schools so children could experience the life cycle of chickens. We at Lab took advantage of this wonderful opportunity and my part was to pick up the eggs for the other kindergarten teachers who, in return, took over week-end responsibilities for me. (We all knew how to share.) Here's how it worked. Though the eggs and the feed were free, the incubator, thermometer, heat lamp, and water bottles were not. I was fortunate to have my budget pay the bill for these items that were cared for and reused for years.

On the morning of the egg pick up, my husband and I drove to the U of I office where we signed out and were given five dozen fertilized eggs (one dozen for each of our kindergarten classes) along with bags of feed. In preparation teachers had to have set the correct temperature in their incubators, usually the day before we delivered the eggs. The instructions stated each egg was to be turned three times a day for all but the last of the full 21 days required for the embryos to develop and the chicks to hatch. (Two of the daily egg turnings were done by children. I did the third turning for the day before leaving for home.)

We shared books that beautifully described the day-by-day embryo development, and contained wonderful pictures of the amazing development from fertilized eggs to live chicks. The kids had seen and many had carefully checked out the incubator, the thermometer, and the lights. Questions were raised and answered before we actually began this amazing involvement.

The most time-consuming part of the preparation was creating an Egg Turning Chart. It required each child's name and time, and day that a child was responsible for turning the eggs from "X" to "O" or "O" to "X". (I had very carefully marked each egg with a letter on either side so they were easily identified.) The nine o'clock child checking the list knew to turn every "O" egg over, and the second turner at one o'clock knew to turn every "X" egg. The chart covered nineteen days, with two children turning each day, along with my turning, up until two days before the hatching was to occur when we were to not disturb the eggs. Supervising, but not interacting too much, was an essential part of this project. How better to help little children become independent.

During those turning days we candled the eggs—holding an egg over a flashlight allowed children to see the development of the embryos inside the shell. The pictures in our books looked just like what was taking place on the 4th, the 8th, 12th, and 16th days of the development. There were some eggs that had nothing but yolk and whitish liquid inside. I opened them and explained they were most likely not fertilized—a rooster had to help make the egg that was in

were stuck to their little bodies once they were out of the shell. The warmth of the incubator dried them and while resting there they became little balls of yellow fluff.

In just two days the chicks were removed from the incubator and put in a sturdy cardboard box that supported the heat lamp. By this time, the chicks were strong enough that children could touch them. Many children gathered around the box watching as chicks climbed, scrambled over each other, fell down and dropped off to sleep only to awaken and begin their "play" again. Once the chicks were four or five days old children were able to gently pick them up and hold them and even give them the freedom to walk around in a large space in the classroom. I isolated their exploring area so I only cleaned poop up from one place and not from the entire room. Once little wings began to sprout, they needed more space so they could attempt at flying and it was then time to say goodbye. A colleague transported all the peeping chicks in a large crowded cardboard box back to the University Extension office where they were then to be taken to farms to live out their lives—or so we were told.

Hatching chicks year after year was a delightful experience with the exception of one year when, over a weekend, the electricity to the incubator was disconnected accidentally, cooling it to a dangerously low temperature. Our unhatched eggs never made it, the embryos all died. The Monday morning I discovered the temperature failure, I explained to the children that we would not have chicks even though everyone had so diligently and carefully cared for them, because, by mistake, the electricity was shut off and chicks were unable to develop in a cold incubator. This wasn't an easy time for any of us.

Children in the other kindergartens heard of our sad mishap and offered to share some of their babies. Eight little chicks were delivered to our room out of the generosity of other kindergarten children. What was at first a very sad situation turned to be a wonderful lesson in helping others, learning to be empathetic and caring.

Empathy is not easy to explain to very young children, but here's one other way I found to do just that. Our community, as in many parts of cities, has homeless people living on the streets. I wasn't surprised when after we passed a man sleeping on a bundle on top of newspapers on the sidewalk where we were taking a walk, homelessness became the focus of our conversation. As soon as we returned to school a child questioned who was this man, why did he sleep outside? Another child said his Daddy said there were people he called homeless. Of course, I was asked what "homeless" meant. From this began many conversations about how fortunate we were to live in houses or apartments—no one lived in a tent or an igloo, but these kinds of dwellings were brought up in our discussion.

When I talked about some children who lived with their mothers in places called shelters more questions were raised. "Where do these kids sleep?" "Do they have stories read before they are kissed goodnight?" "Who cooks their dinner? "These were only a very few of the questions that needed answers, and so began a year-long project.

I located a shelter for women and children not too far from our campus and thought that families could bring clean, wearable clothing and household items to school (We had our corner just outside our room where they could be collected, and volunteer parents could deliver them to the shelter.) Children said they had lots of toys and books they didn't need anymore and their families had things they could share too. An explanatory letter brought not only volunteer drivers, but boxes and bags of wonderful items that soon filled the hallway corner.

On delivery day, children made a line and passed a bag or box they could handle from one child to the next to empty the pile and load the delivery car: a human conveyor belt.

As Thanksgiving approached Anne asked if there would be a big Thanksgiving Dinner at the House. Ah, another opening for me to use. I asked if there were jobs these children could do at home to earn nickels or pennies they'd bring to school and we could send some special food along with the bags of important items. Ideas for earning money poured forth—a child might empty the dishwasher, match socks into pairs, help set a table, clear dishes, and for sure there were many other jobs to be done.

We had a big jar that could hold the coins and together we made a list of what jobs had been done; many new ideas for earning money were shared. As the jar filled, these coins became well used every day. Children emptied the coins and sorted pennies, nickels, dimes and an occasional quarter. In no time most children recognized and could name each of the coins. There were several children who demonstrated that five pennies was the same as a nickel, and many times I was asked why a dime that could buy more was smaller than a penny?

The week before Thanksgiving I asked for ideas about sending so many coins in a bag to the Home. "Let's send a check" said an almost five year old which led to yet another important conversation. I know I wasn't successful in explaining checks, but when I said the neighborhood bank, in walking distance, could help change our coins everyone was eager to go. I walked to the bank after school and set up the date to have the coins counted so that the bank then would give us a check for that amount. (Children had counted and counted and always came up with a different amount, we needed a money counting machine to do the job.)

Our little wagon carried our well wrapped jar of coins. Once at the bank we were greeted by a lady, who told us she was a cashier, who ushered the children to where the counting coin machine was situated. Everyone gathered round it. Dropping all the money into the machine was noisy and even noisier when the machine began to do its job. The cashier said the machine counted $16.24 and she would make a bank check to the Home for that amount of money— the bank would keep the coins, and we'd send the check in time to buy a Thanksgiving Turkey. (I couldn't tell if this whole process seemed understood, but no one voiced an objection.)

With each car load delivered, our volunteer parent brought back a note thanking the children for their caring. On receiving the check, there were child-made drawings and many handwritten notes of thanks.

The collecting and earning coins went on through the year, and once again the jar filled.

I explained I received mail from many places that needed money to accomplish their important helping work and I had to decide where and what need I would help. I had learned that a father of two children at Lab had died and there was a fund being set up to help pay for their schooling. I told the children this sad need and asked what we might do to help. "Vote, we should vote about this"; and that is what we did. It was decided the coins should be taken to the bank and the bank lady should make the check for the family without the daddy. We did just that.

One afternoon, while sitting at one of the little tables catching up on some paper work a woman appeared at our classroom door. I had never seen her before, but somehow thought she might be the new widow. She introduced herself and over our cups of tea, with tears in her eyes she managed to tell me there had been support from many places, but she was so very touched to know little children cared enough to send her money for her children.

We kept in touch. I watched her two boys grow. When the oldest completed eighth grade, I attended his graduation, seated next to his mother. By the time the youngest boy was to enter high school their mother had remarried, and this very sad story was completely changed.

Now, those boys are men, and this happily married woman and I sometimes meet in the neighborhood grocery store, to hug and chat.

I had to include this story taken from so many happenings that have remained important during my years of teaching.

University Involvements

Another plus of being a teacher at Lab put me right on the University campus with its many exciting places to explore and to visit with children. A small body of water, Botany Pond, in walking distance from our classroom, was drained each fall and its fish were housed in huge tanks in the adjacent Botany building. I, once again, did my homework, and made the needed contacts to find out when the fish would be removed and housed indoors in one of the labs. I explained to a friend whose office was adjacent to the Pond that my Lab School class could care for many fish over the winter months, and with her help, we planned a field trip to the Pond.

Children took notes home asking permission to "fish-sit" for the winter, and the families who thought it a good idea responded positively and sent a large-necked plastic bottle with a lid along with a plastic bag to school. We put two clean empty large buckets in the wagon and walked to the Botany building where the fish were housed in huge tanks. With just enough water to keep fish submerged we watched as my friend caught many fish in her net and dropped them into our buckets for the careful trip back to school. Once in our room all the fish went into our 20 gallon tank and with our net I fished out one or two fish for each "fish-sitter" depending on their parents' notes. We were left with more than enough fish for the classroom tank.

The pond fish that remained in the classroom provided a soothing quiet experience as children pulled a chair next to our tank to watch them swimming, or going to the top of the water to feed. Many observations were made (some fish swam way down at the bottom of the tank, others in the middle), and there were many questions raised by the children.

Ah, but fish tanks need to be cleaned, and emptying 20 gallons was an unpleasant chore for me. Following an impulse, I used our net to capture all the fish and put them in a bucket of clean water, leaving the dirty water in the tank to be emptied. One morning I related an abbreviated version of *The Sorcerer's Apprentice*, a story from *Fantasia*, now the Disney version familiar to most of the children. I proceeded to turn on the record player. The children listened to the music, and saw several small buckets next to the empty dirty fish tank. You can imagine what happened next. I waved a small broom from the dramatic play area (my magic wand) and the Disney tale came to life. Children took on the roles of the Sorcerer's brooms carrying the small buckets I filled with dirty water to the classroom sink where they were dumped, returning them to the tank to be refilled. As the music played, the children pretended, and the tank emptied. In no time at all, the dirty fish tank water was gone, and washing the stones on the floor of the tank, refilling it with clean water was a simple job. A once dreaded task for me became a delightful experience for the children. What fun! (It wasn't until years later that I learned the fishy water would have been great for fertilizing my plants rather than dumping in the sink—too late, too bad.)

The fish that survived the winter in homes, and surprisingly many did, were returned to school in April, in time for Earth Day. These fish were once again put into large buckets, loaded into our little red wagon for the trip back to the newly refilled pond. As the children knelt on the ground on one side of the pond I carefully lowered our container into the water to release the fish to the waters they had come from in the fall. What I hadn't realized was that the pond water was still too cold and instead of the fish swimming away, as expected, the fish touched the water froze and died instantly. The looks on the faces across from me were those of sheer horror. I had to respond quickly and explain that we couldn't do anything to change the sad happening, but we certainly could learn from it. We would never again release fish too early in the spring, but rather we would wait for the water to be warmed by the sun. Fortunately, just then, a Kingfisher bird flew by, and I explained that our mistake would be food for that bird and its family. It helped somewhat, but was for all of us a huge lesson. I certainly had to think on my feet this day—a happening that is repeated often, an essential part of being a teacher.

When problems arose, I tried to find ways to include children in their solutions. Our classroom was fortunate to include a small bathroom that housed two child-sized toilets and a low small sink. Children washed not only their hands in the sink, but at times they washed small sandy toys and paint brushes as well. Here was the problem that needed a way to solve. Too often the P-trap, visible under the sink, clogged with these items, and at times there was an overflow and a flood. I became an expert on piling newspapers on the flood waters to absorb the liquid. After several plumber visits, my husband and I installed a plastic see-through "P" pipe under the sink.

Once this pipe was in place, whenever paintbrushes were washed, children could see the colored water as it flowed under the sink. They were fascinated watching water flow through the see-through pipe—soapy water, at times colored water, but nothing but water went down the drain to the "P" trap. The problem of the trap being clogged with small objects disappeared. Children would place their hands on the pipe and know if it was hot or cold water flowing through it. They could see the colors blend as a yellow and a blue brush were washed.

This was so successful, I wanted to install clear pipes so we could see what happened when toilets were flushed, but no way would the University Plumbers allow feces to move through glass pipes. I did request a see-through toilet and a well-known plumbing supply company sent me a half toilet that unfortunately couldn't be used. Though I tried I was unsuccessful in having a glass panel inserted over an electrical outlet. Only my "P" trap under the sink let children see the results of their actions.

I was delighted to have my article, "Make Holes in the Environment and Let Children See Inside," published. (Please see Appendix A, page 156.)

We certainly expect children will ask questions, many questions. Some of them they actually want to have answered, but some are just a way to make conversations. Adults raise questions, and for me, it was important that the questions asked of children required thought, never just a "yes" or a "no" answer. Wording my query by saying, "Tell me why," "What else could you do"? "How did you figure that out"? "What do you think should happen"? My questions couldn't be brushed off with a nod of a head or a quick single word reply. Conversations sprouted all through the days I was teaching. I loved it.

Everybody in our room helped with caring for the animals and plants we housed. Our classroom had our Reptile, Cleveland, (children also learned from the snakes, on loan, from the woods in Wisconsin and kept for two weeks before returning them), our Mammal, Ginny the Guinea Pig, the Fish from Botany Pond, and the chicks that were with us for just a short period of time. I was excited when a friend offered to give us one of his aviaries along with a pair of zebra finches he had bred. This then completed our classroom menagerie. I've much to share about raising birds but first I want to explain how our animal setting became part of a doctoral study.

Because children in my classroom lived with, studied, fed, cared for and learned about this wide range of animal life, a graduate student, Olin Eugene Myers, spent an entire year in my classroom collecting material for his doctorate, *The Developmental Basis of an Ecological Self.*

I re-met Gene one evening while I was at the neighborhood copying store. He had visited my class room weeks before and one evening while I was duplicating some papers in the neighborhood shop, he approached me to talk about his interest in young children and animals. Our conversation went on for so long, I invited him to continue talking about his plans over tea in my kitchen. That very evening we agreed he'd come to my room the following day to see how he could involve children and their interactions with our animals to gain the data required for his doctoral research.

As planned, I introduced Mr. Myers to the children and told them that because they were all wonderful pretenders, everyone was to pretend he was invisible until the time that he was ready to be part of our room. He spent two "invisible" weeks learning names, observing interactions, before he started being involved with children in small groups, and with individual children.

For the entire school year, Mr. Myers came each day, collecting his data through many different means. He met with the children's parents in my home one evening explaining his work plan and asking for them to participate by keeping specific records related to their child's conversations about their interactions with him at school. Families were very cooperative and helpful.

Gene's presence became part of our environment, his involvement with children completely accepted. His work included small group conversations, observations of children with our many animals. In the last weeks of the school year he had a variety of animals brought into the room—a boa constrictor snake, a dog, a monkey, a tarantula, to mention a few, and he and the owners of the animals raised and answered the children's specific questions.

Organizing his vast collection of notes and then writing took him several years. I was honored to have been invited to attend the session where, in front of a distinguished group of University of Chicago Professors, Gene Meyers defended his dissertation. He later published his findings in a book (See the bibliography) *Children and Animals: Social Development and Other Connections to Other Species*, 1998. In 2007 a second edition was printed, *The Significance of Children and Animals: Social Development and Our Connection to Other Species*, using the data gathered from my classroom, along with significant findings from other experts in this new and growing field of research. In both books the children's names were changed, as was mine-- my nomenclature was Mrs. Ray. When his first book was published, I sent print releases to all the families whose children were involved in Gene's study so they could purchase their own copies of the first edition. (I had long been retired when his second book was published) Dr. Myers is now a Professor of Environmental Studies at Huxley College, Western Washington University in Bellingham, Washington. The year he spent in my room was wonderful for all of us, and to think it began because we talked while copying pages needed for school. What a great involvement–how special to be a significant part of a doctoral study.

Over the years we have kept in touch. My husband and I attended Gene's wedding and when their first child was born the announcement read—"We can furnish clothing and toys for our baby girl, but what we cannot be sure is that we will be able to give her an unspoiled outdoor environment, so if you would, please donate to a conservation area in Bellingham or other natural place." Since then, we have often donated to *World Wildlife*, and *Nature Conservancy* (two of our favorites) rather than send a material gift for a newborn. A grand idea suggested by our friend, Dr. Myers.

One morning, children were alarmed to hear a thump made when a small bird flew into our classroom window, fell to the ground and lay there unmoving. We talked about it possibly having broken its neck and it was agreed, after observing its unmoving, still little body that it was dead. Some children said we should bury it in the play yard, an idea that sounded good to many. I commented that a bird carcass (and I used that word) might possibly attract bugs and rodents, or, by accident, be dug by an unsuspecting child one day. Since ours was not the only class playing in the outside space, I wondered how children felt about using the yard as an animal cemetery. They had to think about this, since I wouldn't accept a response of "Yes" or "No." My words stirred up a variety of conversation so I suggested before the day was over, we'd revisit the topic to see if there was another thing to do besides burying it in the yard. It was important and we did continue the conversations later that same day giving children time to think through to a solution.

While waiting for children's to offer their ideas for solving the question of what to do with the little bird, I wrapped it and placed it in the freezer section of our small classroom refrigerator. That afternoon serious little children gathered on the rug eager to find out what might be the best way to handle the problem of "what to do with the little dead bird." At the start of this talk we did affix photos of owls to the glass, hoping they would make our windows safe and other birds would stay away from the owls. Following this positive action, many ideas were expressed, and it was clearly THE solution when a child suggested that maybe the bird could become part of the Academy Museum. A few weeks prior to finding the dead bird, we had taken a field trip to the Chicago Academy of Sciences which, years later, was renamed the Peggy Notebaert Nature Museum. We had seen bird specimens in their exhibits. This was a perfect idea, but it required a phone call to the Director to explain the problem of disposing of a found dead bird. The then director, Paul Heltne, was very cooperative. He said to bring the frozen bird to the Academy, but before coming, the children were to research and identify it, and I, representing the children, would need to sign a paper giving the Museum permission to add it to their bird collection for their scientists to study. (A second dead bird children discovered was also to be taken to the Academy.)

The children found, through looking at bird books from our school library, that one bird was a Common Yellowthroat, the other a Brown Creeper. In only a few days the anticipated paper giving the Museum the rights to the specimens arrived. I signed it after having shared the information with the children and we planned our second trip to the Academy. The Director met us at the entrance, took the paper I had signed along with the little box that held the dead, frozen birds and verbally thanked the children for their contribution to the Museum collection for study and research. But, before we left the Museum (we stayed on and explored) the director did more: he presented me with an official certificate thanking the children in my pre-school class for the birds that would become an addition to their collection. On that same afternoon, once back at school, I made copies of THE CHICAGO ACADEMY OF SCIENCES CERTIFICATE:

THE CHICAGO ACADEMY OF SCIENCES

gratefully acknowledges the receipt of

one Brown Creeper (Certhia americana) specimen

and

one Common Yellowthroat (Geothlypis trichas) specimen

A GIFT TO THE MUSEUM OF NATURAL HISTORY

from   Ms. Needlman's pre-school class from the
University of Chicago Lab School

Paul S. Helton
Director.

Chicago, Illinois

The Trustees of the Academy accept this gift on the understanding that it is unrestricted and offered without limiting conditions.

On the following day I presented a certificate to each child. Everyone in the class was delighted to have an official paper to take home. Once the excitement of the ownership of such a document subsided, it was time that I carefully explained, should a child find other dead birds, these were the only ones needed at the Museum. I could imagine how families would have responded to a collection of dead birds in their freezers. I wanted to be certain I didn't leave bird collecting open ended to avoid any problems with it in the future.

Some Fly Some Slither

Now, back to birds in my classroom living in our aviary that over the years housed and was the place where zebra finches, then canaries, and mourning doves were our final occupants were raised.

A pair of Zebra Finches were gifted to us as their needs were few and they were prolific even for a novice like me. I stumbled upon a wonderful bird shop, thanks to the Yellow Pages, and along with the shop's owner figured out that in the fall I would purchase a pair of birds, and at the end of the school year in June, I would deliver our initial couple and any offspring to his shop, and he, the following fall, would give me another pair and their needed food supply making an even financial exchange. This great plan worked for many years.

There was much to be learned from this beautiful addition to our room. We talked about the plants, the feeding and water dishes that I placed on the cage floor, the perches and the nesting basket I hung in the aviary before birds were introduced. It was agreed that bird watchers would use eyes only so as to not disturb the birds except when it was time for children to poke nesting materials—strings, bits of cotton, shredded paper the birds would haul in their beaks into the nesting basket—then they could use hands as well.

On most days children sat on the floor in front of the aviary so they could watch the birds. It was exciting when a child called out to come and watch when, for the first time, the male Finch worked at stuffing the nesting materials into the basket and the female disappeared inside, maybe to do some arranging. (The sex of Zebra Finches was easy to identify—the mature male had orange cheek markings, the female's cheeks were unmarked.) The birds took turns being inside the nesting basket. When they flew to eat, leaving the nesting basket exposed, another observant child announced there were tiny jelly bean shaped eggs in amongst the string and nesting stuff. A few children counted the little eggs, and we decided to start record keeping: the number of eggs and the date they were discovered.

The floor in front of the aviary was constantly occupied as children watched and waited, but nothing happened. An explanation of what was wrong with the eggs had to be told. Most of the bird watchers knew it was the female's job to lay eggs—raising chickens had been the source of this information and chickens are birds. The information that was needed to be repeated was the role of the male who had to help make the eggs if there were to be babies (more sex info for children). Finally, after numerous eggs were seen and the male and the female kept taking turns sitting on them, high-pitched sounds came from the basket. The eggs hatched!

At each step of the process, the children dictated and I recorded their observations—time for nest building, mating. One child had seen the male mount the female; now children knew a part of conception that many parents questioned: "How *are* eggs fertilized?" Once some of the eggs had hatched both bird parents were busy caring for their young—eating seeds and putting their beaks into the little open mouths of the offspring. The babies made squawking sounds that we interpreted as "feed me, feed me" and stuck their little very bald, somewhat ugly heads out of the nesting basket.

Though children fed the other animals in our room, I made it my job to feed our birds since the aviary door had to be opened when food and water dishes were to be washed and/or filled. Having birds flying in the room wasn't a good idea and we avoided it from happening.

One day children noticed that the crop, a pouch in the tiny necks of the baby chicks, looked bumpy, unhealthy and strange. I had no idea if our birds were ill. We tried to find information from our books but with no luck. A few children accompanied me to the office to phone the local Zoo Ornithology Department. (No cell phones in those days, we had to go to the school office to place a call.) The ornithologist, Kevin Bell, explained that the crop is where the eaten seeds first are stored before being digested but when the chick's feathers grow as the birds mature, the crop will no longer be visible. Everyone was pleased to learn that our babies were neither deformed, nor terribly ill. Our little birds were healthy. It was important to realize when we were unable to locate the answer to the health question from any of our books we could go directly to an expert. Today children would have gone directly to the Internet for the needed information, but the zoo was the perfect place to find our answers. (Dr. Bell is now the Director of Lincoln Park Zoo in Chicago.) My article for an educational publication, "Raise Birds to Raise Questions" was published, (please see Appendix B, page 160.) and I brought a copy of the magazine article to the bird shop. The shopkeeper, who had been somewhat distant and not overly friendly, invited me to his upstairs apartment for a glass of wine and let his very special parrot sit on my arm—he now understood why I raised his birds in my classroom.

Our plan of paying for the first bird couple continued for years until the shop closed. For many school years we had been fortunate to have several baby birds to return, along with their parents when school closed in June. In September, a food supply and a new couple were ours at no cost. It was indeed a perfect arrangement,

Without access to our first bird shop, I sought out another supplier. This next experience involved a feed store that sold a variety of birds. I selected two mourning doves to breed. Their mournful calls attracted me and were a source of great recall for many parents as they visited and recognized sounds from their childhood. Again, I made the same exchange arrangements: I paid for the original couple, and then exchanged the offspring at the close of school for another pair of birds and the needed food supply the following fall. From this new supplier we raised mourning doves for several years and then followed with canaries that enchanted us with their beautiful songs. All in all, raising birds was a wonderful learning experience for children, teachers as well as families. Many days it was our aviary and singing or peeping birds that attracted the children's attention and quieted any loud voices so the bird sounds could be heard. (Weekends didn't present any problems, but I had to make arrangements for caring for the birds over week long holiday periods and that wasn't always easy.)

I've described some of the animals that lived in our room and they were nothing out of the ordinary but housing snakes was a different story. For periods of no more than two weeks, a garter snake lived in our room, a second reptile other than Cleveland the toad. We tried to provide it with a variety of foods, but it never ate while in captivity. Two weeks was long enough for the children who wanted to hold it to become comfortable with snake before I returned it to the woods where it had been found. No harm was done to the snake that lived without food for the brief two week time. While living at school, almost every child moved from "not me" to touching, and even to holding it with comfort.

Sometimes I was fortunate to locate a different harmless snake to bring into our room for the children to research and identify through books from the library. (Remember, children from a university community like ours loved "research.") It was a snake that had children feeling really powerful once they were confidently holding it. To my amazement there were several teachers who were very uncomfortable and verbal about disliking the reality of a snake, even a harmless one, being in the building. I explained to children that if these teachers had known snakes when they were young, they would not be concerned or afraid as adults.

Strange Places Lead to Science Learning

———•———

Finding food for animals was sometimes a challenge. As for food and children, we did a great deal of cooking and eating.

I didn't have the funds to purchase an oven from my classroom budget, but my request to the Parents' Association made it happen. My room provided a safe place close to an electrical outlet that became the permanent home for a small convection oven which was shared with the other Nursery-Kindergarten classes. Any class that used it returned it clean and ready for the next project which might be baking, changing solids to liquids, drying wet snow pants or soggy shoes (the very lowest setting did a great job of removing moisture) and it was small enough to wash thoroughly if it had been used for anything other than foods. With almost a straight face, I'd tell children we'd have dried socks for snacks on a snowy day—it took a moment before everyone understood I was joking.

Some, not all, children had a beginning understanding of evaporation when I'd put a small pan of water into the oven, and steam vapors, water droplets appeared on the glass door and then disappeared, evaporated. When wet mittens in the oven left drops of moisture on the oven's glass door, and the mittens were dried: evaporation. Using the oven, a versatile piece of equipment, involved great vocabulary building and certainly facilitated beginning science concepts. Words were not always necessary to get across a point since some children were careful observers and answered their own questions. I encouraged, taking time to look and figure out what was happening, what was taking place, and then, when needed I would put into words what they had observed. I always felt it was so special to be with little children as they grew, learned, and taught me to look and listen to their actions and words. Being a teacher was always exciting—never a dull moment.

Science learning took place while having snacks. Some days I put out our frozen mixed vegetables and they were served in two ways: frozen or cooked. Children were delighted to put a frozen, hard, round pea into their mouths and wait until it softened. Those same veggies slowly dried in our convection oven became hard, delicious, crispy, unusual finger foods. Children who would not touch any food known to be a vegetable loved eating them. Of course I shared these ideas with families in a newsletter which I sent home weekly, safety-pinned to the children's backs. Imagine enjoying vegetables!

Following simple picture instructions printed on cards for measuring ingredients were required for some recipes. At times "cooks/bakers" put the ingredients they thought would make delicious cookies—butter, sugar, chocolate chips, milk, eggs into a bowl, seldom if ever accurately measured. Several of these creations were actually edible. Children observed soft foods could become hard, e.g., eggs were liquid when first opened but when cooked, became hard, but, some hard ingredients become soft, e.g., butter, when heated or refrigerated changed from solid to liquid. What discoveries!

All of us, children and teachers used the convection oven, the tiny freezer space on the top of the little refrigerator, or sometimes just the cold out of doors to change foods, bake them, and/or dry them. We talked about where the flour came from that was used in most baking recipes, and that led us to exploring wheat seeds, and even grinding them to make flour. This was not a great success. Science activities sprung up in unforeseen places and I tried not to miss any. Whenever there were oranges in a child's lunch their seeds were collected and when dried (it took a day or two once seeds were spread on a paper towel) they were planted in little pots. The seeds were carefully watered, placed in our south facing window to capture the sunlight, and in a short time, they germinated. The tiny orange plants never grew beyond an inch or two, but it was exciting to see a stem appear, and tiny leaves open.

Children also collected their apple seeds, but they required a long period of dormancy and cold before they would germinate. For many years there were little containers of apple seeds in the refrigerator for the entire winter with the idea that they would be planted in the spring. Somehow, we never carried through on this planting. Who could remember? For us, only the orange seeds germinated. (Sometimes we were successful with grapefruit seeds and they did germinate but the little plants too grew gangly and died.) Our only successful germinating results were from citrus fruit seeds.

When stickweeds appeared everywhere in our playground and children were finding them painful, something had to be done. Rather than wait for the custodial crew to remove the plants, teachers, wearing gloves, tackled them—five huge bags were filled on our "stickweed working removal days." Questions were raised, "What do these plants do?" "How come so many grow?"

Before beginning book research, children carefully opened several of the prickly things to discover that the small fine prickles were protecting little plants within the tiny seeds. This experience launched a scientific investigation of how the seeds were planted, and a whole awareness of seeds in the environment, at a four and five year old level of understanding of course. What part of children's lunches held seeds? What shapes do seeds take? There are some very large seeds and very tiny ones, what does the size tell us about the plant? To find answers to some of these questions we walked through the community collecting seeds from dried flowers (many were used for collage creating in the art area, some were planted.) From this year-long work grew my article that was printed in *Learning Magazine*, 1982, "Seeds of Preschool Science." (Please see Appendix C, page 165.)

Ears of dried field corn, each kernel being a seed, were piled into the dry "water/sand table" and children worked hard to remove the kernels from the cobs. A pile of the kernels, covered with a heavy towel to be safe, were pounded with a hammer and the cracked seeds put outside to feed wild birds. Some corn kernels were counted or their number estimated when they filled a clear container, some made strange bumpy roads for small cars to drive through while covering the bottom of the dry "water table". There were the occasional kernels that somehow found a little moisture and within a few days sprouted, or germinated. Whenever we found sprouts children fed them to our guinea pig, or put them into the aviary for our birds. Experiencing corn kernels in many ways utilized math and science knowledge—it was part of playful learning that children were exposed to in our classroom. We did more corn cracking which you'll find on the pages I share on Human Rights and little children.

Once a month, a small committee of children met with me or an assistant teacher to decide on a simple menu and figure out the ingredients needed for making lunch and with an adult's help made a shopping list. With it in hand, a teacher and the children, on the morning of their cooking day, walked to a nearby small grocery store, bought the items needed and prepared the food—e.g., pizza with English muffin as crusts, tomato sauce with cheese for the topping; macaroni and cheese, pancakes with turkey bacon, accompanied by a fresh fruit or vegetable and a choice of juice, hot chocolate or cold milk. (After I retired, the little grocery store closed, and our lunch program would have had to make other shopping arrangements.)

Menus were written with inventively spelled words; the tables were washed and set ready for a special meal. The cooking committee printed invitations to come to lunch that were delivered to our Principal, the Music, the Physical Ed teacher or one of the librarians— depending on the amount of food prepared. If I had to explain the rationale for this particular activity I would have explained it as an example of how Literacy and Science were connected in our room, but I never had to justify my program.

One of my many classrooms I occupied was located at the end corner of the long first floor hallway. (This space, large enough to house the bags brought to share with the Home left room for a special table where I'd set up interesting "science" materials.) Children and parents walking into school stopped to see what was on the "Science Table". The first such table I made out of a wide board held up by two hollow blocks. I was able to replace it, after my grant proposal was accepted and I was given a small stipend. Having some funds the make-shift table became a "museum". Up to this time the items I needed to purchase were paid for from my purse—as is the case, unfortunately, with many expenses we teachers encounter.

I designed and my husband built a wonderful hexagon table with a white top. Two sides, of this hexagon, covered small shelves slightly raised off the floor, where two exhibit cases borrowed from the Field Museum's Harris Loan Collection were displayed. The underside of the tabletop provided lighting for these cases, and a three-pronged fixture hung over the table from the ceiling. Red, blue, and green stage light filters covered these lights so children could blend colors, make shadows in duplicate or triplicate depending on where their hands or some objects were placed on the white six-sided cabinet top. Some days the lighting was uncolored, easily done by the flick of its switch.

The plastic tube fastened to the back of the table top allowed children to rub a cloth and make tiny plastic particles dance around---static electricity. It helped explain the electric shock, static electricity, children often encountered in a very dry environment or what kept a rubbed balloon fastened to clothing or to a wall—static electricity.

On the backside of the table was an enclosed storage area. In it I housed animal skins, skulls, bones, photographs, owl pellets, and dozens of other wonderful specimens that I collected, rotated and coordinated with the content of the Museum exhibit cases. These incredible Museum cases were exchanged and replaced with new ones every three weeks. Early in the fall of each year, I selected from the Museum's extensive collection, a full year of borrowing. In the first year I made the trips to the Field Museum to pick up the cases, at times my husband did the returning and/or picking up, and until I finally involved parent volunteers to make the trek. My borrowing list allowed the Museum staff to give the person picking up the case the one I had selected, or make a substitute if a teacher from another school hadn't returned the case as scheduled. It took me several years to learn to delegate jobs—and delegating is really important. Guess I was a slow learner.

In the mornings as families walked their children into school, and all through the day, children and adults stopped to examine the cases interact with objects, e.g. feathers, skulls, bones, etc., or to browse the books from the library that held information related to the exhibit cases available on our Museum table top. Sometimes there was shadow play happening—it was a well-used table.

The year I retired the parents of my last class and parents from many previous classes set up a fund to continue to care for the science corner I created and maintained for so many years. My former families installed a bronze plaque next to the table that read:

THE GLORIA NEEDLMAN SCIENCE CORNER
Honoring the creativity and dedication of an
outstanding Teacher, who, during her thirty three
years of service to the Laboratory Schools, inspired
us to love the earth and to Respect each other.

Dedicated May 31, 1998

Long after my retirement, when I walked through the Laboratory Schools halls on my way to do some research in the extraordinary children's library, or just pay a visit to an old colleague, I'd pass my Science Corner with its bronze plaque. It remained a thrill for me.

A new Earl Shapiro Early Childhood Center replaced the old houses where I first began at Lab, and the room with the wonderful corner space in the big school building that housed my Nursery/Kindergarten classrooms. This new building was built on the site of the abandoned Doctors' Hospital, formerly the Illinois Central Hospital, where so long ago I was born. My Science Corner is now housed in this extraordinary new building. How perfect!

Lending Not Losing

———————●————————

My classrooms, and I did have several different ones over the years, were always filled with books available for children to look at, to "read," or to have read to them. From the first days of each school year I read aloud throughout the day from fiction picture books, for information from some non-fiction, sometimes to the full group, at times to just a few children. Later in the year, depending on the attention span of the group, chapter books were added usually when children spread out on their blankets or cots to rest and relax. (Most young children required a quiet time during the school day making it the perfect venue for aloud reading.) I often found when I reached the end of reading a chapter or two and announced "To be continued" little voices would call out, "Don't stop now. Read some more." What wonderful words! Kids were becoming hooked on books.

Our classroom library borrowing system worked amazingly well. In the back of each book was a glued pocket, and in it I put a card with the name of the book and our room number. Every child had a matching pocket hung on a wall chart that held two identical cards each with the child's name and our classroom number. To borrow a book or two a child had to put the card with the books information in her/his own card pocket, and placed her/his name card in the book to be borrowed. I could just glance at the wall chart and locate every borrowed book. Books left on a school bus or dropped in the hall were identified and returned to our room. This was the closest foolproof lending library system I figured out, one that put the responsibility where it belonged—with the borrowing child. Being responsible had to involve the families of my young children. Before books were ever borrowed I informed them that borrowed books were to be kept only for one week and then returned. It was important books were circulated and borrowed by others. During the year there were some families who required reminder notes that books were kept at home for too long a time and were needed back in our room. (One such note usually brought a book back unless it was lost and then families were charged a replacement fee.)

I've included some of the Titles of chapter books my young children loved in the Bibliography. I was never certain all my families read aloud, shared books, made trips to the library and to book stores, so I made certain books played an important part in the lives of children.

Research endorsed by The American Academy of Pediatrics through the *Reach Out and Read* program (www.reachoutandread.

org) has proven that early literacy means greater school success. If you wonder why I added my plug for ROAR, it is because my son, developmental pediatrician Robert Needlman, founded this program over 20 years ago. I had to mention it as this program puts books into inner city hospital waiting rooms, has volunteers reading to children and has doctors prescribing twenty minutes of reading aloud every day to families. Each child patient chooses a book available in many languages from a large collection which then becomes part of the child's own home library. Sure makes me a proud Mom.

After I'd finished sharing *The Big Friendly Giant,* by Roald Dahl, a great chapter book for youngsters, children created a huge friendly giant from two 8-foot-long pieces of wrapping paper. They took turns drawing his head, shoulders, arms, body and long, long legs. The "Giant" figure was cut out, a big job that took several cutters to complete. The front and the back of the paper giant were fastened together with staples and some needle and thread stitching, leaving room for children to stuff him with sheets of crumpled newspaper. He had to lie on the floor until we borrowed a tall ladder from the building engineer to suspend our giant above our heads. He moved about gently once connected to the high classroom ceiling. This magnificent giant with features, and clothing painted by our artists lived in the room for the remainder of the school year and then found its way to decorate the school library.

We read fiction, we read non-fiction. We discussed characters, plots, and through it all children loved books and all they discovered through them.

The Parent Association sponsored a book swap yearly and children brought books from their homes that they had read and reread and no longer wanted on their shelves. In the classroom each book was exchanged for one chit, (a small piece of cut paper) that was to be used instead of money. The chits were traded for books brought to the swap by others. Every class was assigned a specific time to go to a large room where tables were organized—fiction, with its many subdivisions, non-fiction, and picture books. Children were given their corresponding number of chits and their shopping began. Some children chose the largest books; size was what they wanted for their chits. Others noiselessly settled down on the floor, usually under one of the tables, crowded as the room was, and carefully perused the books before making their decisions. On book swap day, once back in our room, we devoted time to the newly selected books so I read aloud as many as time allowed.

The Book Swap provided more than a way to recycle books. The opportunity it gave children to make their own selections was special. This exchange system certainly involved thinking as children figured out the number of chits they had needed to match the number of books they could choose. Ah, another meaningful place for numbers while opening an opportunity to talk about ways children select books.

Children not only listened to stories but were encouraged to create their very own. A parent volunteer would invite the child who had put her/his name was on the signup sheet, to go from our room to a small table set in the hallway near the Science Center. The child would dictate and the adult would proceed to write down the words just as a child said them. An additional sheet of paper was offered for illustrations. I'd collect the stories, and we'd have a theater time as each "author" or "playwright" chose children to act out the story while the rest of the class became the audience. The stories children told were mostly original ones though sometimes they incorporated ideas taken from movies, TV or from books.

Audience etiquette was important and I stressed it. Children were encouraged to give only positive responses e.g. clapping, and they were instructed to sit quietly during each presentation. The "stories" took but a few minutes to read, and two or three were read at one sitting. I worked at making certain every child had an opportunity to be part of some story, and authors were encouraged to look around and see who hadn't had an acting turn, and invite those children to participate. Who knows how this influenced budding thespians, and playwrights. (My colleague and friend, Vivian Paley, was awarded a McArthur Grant for her books written about story dictation which she did somewhat differently than I did, and she won the grant.)

Adults and children as well enjoy having reading materials available while in the bathroom. I made certain books were in many areas of the classroom, the dramatic play space, the block and art area to name a few, so why not in the bathroom?

The small bathroom within our classroom, the one with its sink see-though P trap, provided enough room for a hollow block to fit between the two commodes. On it I kept a few books accessible and frequently changed. Often two seated children would talk about the stories, and "read" to each other. Whenever I happened to be in earshot I overheard serious conversations about the books, about feelings and about relationships that seemed to only take place in the privacy of the bathroom.

Over the years of teaching, the large hollow blocks and other important items for children working together or alone seemed to grow. A container of small colored blocks, in various shapes were well used, sometimes to embellish a large structure, making it fancy, or as part of a challenging game. This is how the game worked. Two children, seated on opposite sides of a small table would each have a set of duplicate little colored blocks (possibly 4 red squares, 2 blue inclined planes, 3 orange rectangles) separated by an unfolded cardboard screen. One child, while building with the blocks, would verbally explain what she was doing. The other child would follow the instructions placing the blocks as directed, and when his structure was completed would remove the screen and compare the two buildings. Sometimes the table held two identical buildings—other times there were little or no similarities to the builder and the follower's results. The children switched roles and depending on the verbal directions given, new block structures were designed. I was needed to set up this game, but only a very few children chose to play. Talking and following directions were skills that needed to be worked on, and developmentally were beyond the development of these youngsters. Live and learn.

The campus of the University has beautiful flower gardens and has in recent years been officially classified as a Botanic Garden. The Grounds and Plant Department (appropriately named) would dig up beautiful mums and geraniums in the fall of each year. When I was quick enough to contact the department in September, at the opening of school, I was able to collect and bring huge plants to our room that continued to bloom through the winter months. A call to families for their garden plants would have worked as well, but for me was not necessary, I had the campus plantings. Before filling our room with plants, I made sure either they could be sent to homes for families to care for them, or I was available to water them, or there were colleagues who would take turns watering over the long holiday breaks.

Early in December the children and I pruned dormant forsythia branches from around campus and put them in a jar of water in a dark closet. By January when we returned from the holiday break, lovely yellow flowers brightened the dark, dank days of winter. One year an observant four year old said, "Those cold branches think it's spring so they open their flowers up in the warm closet."

Our guinea pig, which the children had named Ginny, was a veggie eater. Children cuddled and fed lettuce brought from home or from their lunch sandwiches to her. Throughout the days a few children would hold and gently stroke "Ginny." Sometimes a child or two created a block maze for her to navigate, or two seated children joined spread out feet and facing each other create an enclosed place where she could really be observed. These interactions along with the responsibility of being careful and caring made the guinea pig a fine addition to the classroom. We never housed little gerbils, as many early childhood rooms do; they move too quickly and can easily disappear under a cabinet, or hurry out an open door.

It was amazing and a complete surprise to me when our guinea pig gave birth to five little pink offspring that looked like wads of bubble gum—all hairless and round. We had only had this "mother" animal for a short period of time, and were unaware she had mated. Surprise! With her cage placed on a table children were able to watch the babies squeeze out of her body, and be licked clean by their Mom. There were wonderful questions to answer after this experience, and what an experience it was. Had we planned it the timing couldn't have been better. I explained that our guinea had mated with the father before she came to live in our room. Mating meant that the father had helped start the growing of guinea babies inside the Mother. It was necessary to have both a male and a female to create a new animal. Another opportunity, one of several, to talk about sex with young children and it was well received especially by little boys. I never was successful to find a book that told about the part of the male in reproduction, so I talked about it.

The chore of purchasing fresh cedar chips for the cage, keeping the water bottle filled, making plans for its care over a holiday week-end, seeing to it that a family invited Ginny Guinea home for a longer break, were all worth the extra time it took.

One year I brought a hedgehog into the room as a replacement for a guinea pig that had died, but it wasn't the best choice of a mammal for little children. We read about its care, and observed it, but it was not cuddly, and being nocturnal, wasn't interested in being active during the school day.

Life and Death Matters

As every teacher knows, you win some and lose some. Death of our guinea pig was not dismissed, but rather it served as an opening for many more Life and Death conversations we had over the year.

I had anticipated there would be a need to discuss death with my little students since we lived with animals. Over time I attended an informative, wonderful workshop presented by Rabbi Earl A. Grollman who pioneered ways to help young children deal with this important part of life. I became familiar with Elizabeth Keebler Ross's book on Dying (she too pioneered her research that dealt with this topic seldom handled well) and I purchased books from a Caring Society that dealt with death of pets, of children, of adults in very kind, gentle, meaningful ways. I found each learning I sought out proved an important help as through my teaching years I had the need to deal with this topic with my young children.

Let me share my story of Suzie and her Daddy's demise. He had been very ill for most of the school year and in the spring he died. She was a four year old with a very wise Mother who had been preparing her little daughter for what was an inevitable circumstance. At the time of Dad's death I thought it could be important, as a non-family member, to be available if needed.

The day of the funeral I went to their home to be with Suzie, as her mother thought it best that she not attend the service. Suzie told me her daddy was so sick he could not ever get better as she cuddled in my lap to read stories, and play with one of her dolls. We talked about all the chairs sent by the funeral parlor and all the people who would be coming to her house remembering and being sad because her Daddy was no longer alive. Some grown-ups might even cry. I stayed with Suzie until she moved off my lap to sit with a family member.

Suzie didn't come to school for two weeks following the funeral. During those days I quietly met with a few children at a time and explained that Suzie's Daddy had died and she and her Mommy needed to be home together but that she would soon come back to school.

The morning she was to return, I was unsure of how to handle her initial entry. I had no clue as to what I would say or do. Suzie and her mother stood together at the bottom of the staircase on their way to our second floor classroom when a classmate, standing at the top of the steps shouted down—"Your Daddy is dead, but mine is alive." I felt weak. What was there to say or do after those harsh words were spoken? While holding her Mother's hand, Suzie proceeded up the stairs, and when she reached the top, she looked relieved. She too must have wondered how she would handle this enormous information, but now it was said and she could move on. This open blunt way was hardly how I ever thought I'd deal with the death of a parent, but in Suzie's case it worked.

One evening, another year, I received a phone call from Ezra's mother with horrible news. His father, an electrical engineer, that day, had been electrocuted while at work. As soon as school ended I drove to their home planning to be with Ez and possibly help in some way. There had been no time for preparation for this fatal accident. When I arrived I learned he had been sent to his aunt's home and had not been told of his father's death. I soon understood he was not included in the mourning process, not part of the shared family sadness.

Ezra's mother did not send him back to school. There was no opportunity for him to talk with his me or classmates, only an abrupt change in his entire world. I wanted to stay in contact with the family, but was unable to reach them. This ending was something I have always regretted. I do so hope he is OK.

According to everything I read and learned it is essential to include a child in the sad parts of a family as well as the pleasant, happy ones. But, each family must decide for themselves, and my input was not asked for from this family.

During yet another school year the mother of my little kindergarten child, J, was diagnosed with terminal cancer. This Mother planned for her inevitable death, a horrible job at best. She set up meetings with me and our Guidance Counselor to talk about what roles she wanted us to fill to offer protection for her little five year old daughter.

I visited J's home when her Mom was no longer able to walk on her own, and J asked me if I knew about her Mom's sickness. "Did I know ALL about it?" I said, "Yes, I did, I knew." I told J whenever she wanted to sit on my lap, talk to me, if ever she needed anything, I would always be available for her.

In the weeks that followed, there were times that J talked about her "very sick" Mom, and children asked if she was going to die. When J was unable to answer, she would come to sit with me and together we explained that no one really knew the answer, but that doctors were trying to help her to live.

Early on the morning of her Mom's death, her daddy called and said J would be coming to school on the bus. I told him I'd be at the curb to meet the bus, something I had not done before. As she took her first step through the bus door onto the sidewalk I learned that during the ride, another child had announced to all the bus riders that J's mom was dead. I took her hand and we took a walk in the courtyard before going into our room. (How special to have assistant teachers who were very capable and could begin the day with the other children without us.) While we walked, hand in hand I asked if she wanted to tell the children about her sadness, or did she want me to tell them. She nodded her head. With J seated on my lap, I explained that there are some very bad sicknesses that doctors cannot help, and it was that bad sickness called cancer that J's Mom had and she could not get better. The conversation and questions were not confined to this death but about the death of one of our animals, about a grandmother's death. My role was to listen, and to reassure that most people live long lives.

There were times during the weeks that followed that J was given a special job, a second turn, or an extra cookie. One of the children said it wasn't fair, so I explained that maybe this was a time to do extra things for J since not having a Mom wasn't fair and J might need more special things now. The children were quiet, and then a child spoke up and said, "That's really fair, and J should have extra stuff at school to help her." How proud I was that my little kindergarten children – they on some level under- stood.

During the last months of her life, I had promised J's mom I would watch her little girl grow and I've kept my word. Through the years J's dad and brother, together with my husband and I, shared dinners and at times breakfasts. For the first Mothers' Day without her mom, we chose a restaurant that the children enjoyed, and hopefully it helped soften that day. Years passed, the family moved away when J was a seventh grader, no longer a student at Lab, her dad remarried, and my husband and I attended their wedding. We were the only school faculty members invited.

When J was a high school junior, we visited their suburban home, and together the two of us planned a Kindergarten reunion at my house. It was understandable that her kindergarten memories were lost or blocked. We put together a list of children to invite, and five girls, now young ladies, responded. They came to our house, made pizza, ate and giggled for hours.

Our relationship has been wonderful, and one that was more important to J in those early years.

J asked me to write a letter of recommendation for her college applications, and to my delight, she was thinking of going into Early Childhood Education. How wonderful to be a teacher of little children. Though I may be retired, my continued involvement with my families knows no bounds.

Over the years I handled several death traumas, but they were not all connected with loved ones, and fortunately they didn't all occur while I had the same group of children. Let me tell you about what took place while Nursery/Kindergarten children were outdoors playing. For me this particular happening was insightful in understanding what children understood about death at the tender ages of three, four and five years.

After a warm spring rain, the play yard was too muddy, but the tennis court nearby looked to have a clear enough surface for running and playing. When we walked onto the court, its surface was covered with "dead" worms. Children ran from one worm to the next seemingly confused that there were so many still bodies. (I knew rain could force worms out of the ground, but I never expected the court surface to be such a place.) I picked up as many of the worms as I could hold and in the warmth of my hand, one, than two, then several more began to move. "Look," children shouted, "They came alive!" Before leaving the scene, girls and boys scurried from one "dead" worm to another gathering as many as we could hold to take indoors.

Our conversations continued inside and with children gathered on our rug with the worms on a paper in the center of our circle, I asked how anyone could tell if a worm was alive or dead. One response was, "First it was dead then it came alive again." Another child said, "No, it was just tired and resting, it isn't dead." A third child said, "When my grandpa died, he couldn't get alive again." Many other children contributed their important ideas, and while we talked, several more of the "dead" worms moved. When there was a quiet period with no further ideas or questions spoken, I asked what they had observed about a worm being alive or dead. Ideas poured forth and I repeated their words, adding mine. When an animal like a worm or any living creature could no longer move any part of its body by itself, could not take in air or breathe, then was it dead of resting? The room was quiet, this was a huge idea to understand, and children pondered my words. Everyone stopped talking to watch worms that were wiggling around on the paper and it was decided they might just have been very cold and still, but when warmed up, they were again able to move and were alive. This idea seemed reasonable and acceptable for what was being observed.

Children separated the live worms, the ones that moved on their own, from those who were dead and unable to move. We put both the live ones and those that were thought to be dead out in our garden space. We also put several non- moving worms in the plastic bowl for Cleveland, our Toad. As I tapped the bowl from below the two or three of them appeared to move and Cleveland snapped and ate this special treat. Too bad we couldn't keep more of the dead worms, but I didn't want to deal with their decaying odor. So long as the worms moved, our little Toad gobbled them up. (Sorry to have tricked this little pet.)

The child who spoke of her grandpa's death wanted more conversation about death, and that was when I brought out the book, *Lifetimes: The Beautiful Way to Explain Death to Children* by Bryan Mellonie and Robert Ingpen. It presents in a lovely way that "Every living thing has a beginning that is birth, and an ending that is death and the time in between is called living. Some creatures have very brief lives only a few days, others live a long, long time, and so it is with people. Most people live long lives, but whenever they die, the time from their birth until death is their lifetime."

More words of wisdom came from the children along with more questions, and requests for me to read *Lifetimes* maybe just one more time. It was these episodes in the lives of little children that prompted me to write "Matters of Life and Death in a Classroom" published and featured on the cover of *Learning Magazine,* 1984. (Please see Appendix D, page 169.)

Trips Worth Taking Are Worth Repeating

———◆———

Any teacher of little children knows how important it is to read and re-read favorite books and I figured out, it would be good to revisit a favorite field trip. These trips always require additional adult hands for safety reasons, and volunteers, usually parents though sometimes Nannies filled those places. One year, beyond our usual volunteers, I thought our new Principal might love to leave her office and join our class for our nature outing. I wrote her an invitation, (not certain she could read one written by inventive spellers) and two children delivered it. In her reply which she delivered in person, she said she was delighted to join us and was looking forward to going to the Nature Center, spending time with children so they had the opportunity to know her and her to know them.

One day prior to our trip, children dictated suggestions of acceptable behaviors for the bus ride. Each entry was to state what was expected—"No's" were not allowed, our rules always needed to tell what children were to do, stated in a positive way. The following examples worked for us:

> Everyone is to sit on a seat on the bus (so much better than "Don't Stand").

Voices used have to be talking ones ("Don't Yell" was the
way was first suggested then changed).

If the windows got opened, they are to let in breezes,
only sounds go out open windows. (Don't put hands out
the windows—a "no no").

The children also worked out a second set of rules to be followed
once we arrived at our destination.

Just comfortably walk along so long as you can see
Teacher's bright colorful hat.

Walking is the way kids move at the Nature Center,
except when we find the perfect place for running.

With only two easy to follow rules adults wouldn't need to give
too many reminders.

On the morning of our trip, children were handed a cardboard
clipboard with a pencil tied to it, and a paper with a few simple
pictures on it as they boarded the bus. During the drive they were
to put a mark next to the picture of a bridge each time the bus
crossed or went under one. For every sign that said "No Parking", or
indicated the Speed Limit that picture was to receive a tally mark.
The pictures were simply drawn on a page. The bus travelers worked
alone or with a friend and some excitedly called out, "There's a
parking sign." "Did you see the speed limit one?"

When we reached our destination the clipboards were left on
each seat so that on the trip home they were waiting with the page
turned over leaving a blank sheet for drawing—a simple job for an
adult to put the clean sign face-up on each board.

Once we were in the woods it was our parent volunteers who
had a difficult time rewording their comments from "Don't" to
stating what it was children should be doing. (It does take practice

to find positive words when "NO" or "DON'T" are easier to say.)
The Principal refrained from making any negative comments I was
pleased to observe.

On the ride back to school most of the boards were left
untouched. Tired little heads nodded, and almost all the passengers
fell asleep, including some of our adult volunteers. Of course, we
sang while travelling, but having things to look for was a good
activity as it involved great conversations and observations, and kept
hands busy—well worth the time it took to prepare.

We made a return trip to the very same woods the following
spring. This time we carried magnifying glasses for spotting tiny
shoots of green poking through the soil under the decayed leaves,
seeing egg sacks and making other discoveries. There were signs of
new life all around, and the mystery of where to look, what might
there be to see was all so different in this season. To repeat the trip
was wonderful.

Not all trips required extensive planning. We took many senses
walks around the neighborhood—seeing, smelling, feeling, and
listening walks (we left out the tasting part) Each of these trips took
minor prep time—cardboard clipboards for each child were used,
saved and reused. Each board had a pencil attached so a child could
record on it.

For some "Seeing Walks" a cardboard rectangle with a strip of
masking tape with its sticky side out was used to collect specimens
found on the ground—the specimens stuck to the tape, and the
collected items were brought back to school to share and talk
about.

Street sounds were such fun to think about. I always meant to
bring a recording device with us, but that never did happen. Imagine
children being so quiet they could hear a squirrel run up a tree trunk,
or take notice of a bird's call. "Listening Walks" were great!

Planning with the children prior to an excursion, writing the
highlights following the return to school, revisiting the experience

several weeks later made each field trip a valuable part of the school year. Today the work of Reggio Emilio has introduced the concept of "Revisiting"; an idea which I had found to be important to do with youngsters.

We Did Party

Parties and celebrations are special for children but THE most special celebration is a child's birthday. And to personalize it, this is what happened for every Nursery or Kindergarten child. I created a large mat cut from a roll of material, one I bartered for from the Recycling Center—2 bags of crushed juice cans in exchange for the roll of plastic material. Around the perimeter of each birthday mat I printed the months of the year, highlighting the appropriate month for the celebrant. At each child's ceremony, held after lunch on the celebrating day, a new 4 year old was to tell how old she was last year,"3", how old before "3", before "2", before "1". We talked about the number of months that make up a year and how, before she was "1", her age was counted in months. And before a child was 1 month old age was counted by the number of weeks the child was until the she was 1 week old; then the number of days the child was and when she was just 1 day old, we talked about the number of hours the child was until the child was first born. It was huge amount of information, but because it was repeated for each birthday, some children actually understood—They got it! Years, Months, Weeks, and Days down to the hour until it all began with being born. (After the first half dozen birthday celebrations, teachers needed to give little help in the backward counting, the whole idea of the time it takes to become a year older—most children understood.)

Secretly, with my back to the children gathered on the rug for the celebration, I placed a dab of orange paint on my nose. In a magical instant I became the SUN and I slowly turned, until I made one complete circle to signify one full day. It would take 365 days to make a year and because I didn't want to get dizzy turning for a day then a night, I was only the rotating sun for one day. The birthday child then walked from her birthday month marked along the mat as all the children chanted, starting with the celebrant's month, through the remaining 11 months. You had to go through all the months to become a year older—and the names of the months of the year were soon part of every child's vocabulary. (The chanting of months began not in January, but at whatever the month of the child's birthday).

The rest of the party included singing Happy Birthday and blowing out the one candle that was in the center of the non-edible three-layer frosted plaster wooden cake. It looked good enough to eat, but it was made of wood, compliments of my husband. Once the candle was extinguished the celebrant passed a napkin and a cookie, a cupcake, a brownie or other treat brought from home, to each child. The beverage served was a cup of colored water and it was the birthday child who chose the vegetable dye color. For some birthdays we served green water, or even purple.

The birthday mat was rolled up and sent home as a special present along with the birthday cards many children had created during the day for the celebrant. Birthdays take on a special meaning for young children, and it was fun to go the whole route. Our long ceremony held everyone's attention, and the colored water was a big hit.

When school was closed for the summer there were always four or more children whose birthdays fell in late June, July or August. In one of the last weeks of the year we held a joint birthday celebration for these children. A mat was made for each summer birthday child, (if there weren't too many celebrants, we went through the years, months, weeks, days, hours). For all, no matter the number of celebrants, the Happy Birthday song was sung to each celebrant who also chose the color of the water to be served. The non-birthday kids chose one of the goodies from all those brought from home. Of course there were many extras we shared with the adults in the school office, the special area teachers, or the librarians. They loved our summer birthday celebrations, and we did too. As to the colored water, each child picked the color water that was most appealing from those offered.

The year a Jehovah's Witness child, Charles, whose religion did not allow celebrations of holidays or birthdays, was a member of our class, I wanted to find a way for him to be comfortable on these occasions. While meeting with Charles' parents and explaining how birthdays are celebrated, they decided he could be involved in the first part of the birthday celebration, walking through the months and weeks, days and hours, but be excluded from the singing and the eating. I described the following simple idea, and they accepted it. Once the first part of the celebration was completed, Charles would move off to the far end of the room where there was a listening corner and he could wear earphones and listen to a taped story of his choosing and not be involved in the singing and eating. His parents found this solution satisfying. We followed this for a few parties, but I felt uncomfortable that the treats were not shared with him so I met with his parents again. It was decided Charles could choose his treat first thing in the morning when a parent or the birthday child brought the treat to the classroom, and put it in his lunchbox to have at home as just an afternoon snack, not a party treat. We followed this plan which satisfied Charles, his parents, and even made me comfortable.

In our newsletter I informed families that Charles family's religion did not allow him to participate in birthday parties. I shared the same explanation with the children. Several families insisted, regardless, on sending their child's party invitation to Charles.

Though the birthday celebration hurdle for Charles was successfully carried out, there were more celebrations to deal with and we tried to do so. I informed Charles's family ahead of time about each one, allowing them to make the decision to either send him to school or keep him at home.

At the suggestion of the children, we celebrated Johnny Appleseed's birthday. We read about how he planted seeds across the country, so we had to celebrate with a party. Children made Whipped Apple Pudding which everyone enjoyed, and of course we sang. (Charles was off to the listening corner).

Chinese New Year was a holiday celebrated most years. When I had a Chinese child as a member of our class I'd invite the parent to come and share the family customs with us. For many years, we were fortunate to have Dr. Lucinda Lee Katz as our director and she came into our room and told her story of being a little girl living in San Francisco's Chinatown. She arranged for our entire school body to come to the courtyard to watch an authentic Dragon Parade. Some years we created our own dragon parade, and children fed the "dragon" oranges for good luck and each child received a small red envelope with a penny in it. With or without a parade, I read several beautiful storybooks that told about Chinese New Year. (Selected titles are in the Bibliography.) My source for obtaining the little red "luck" envelopes was to purchase them from one of many shops in Chicago's Chinatown.

To celebrate a Chinese custom only once a year wasn't adequate, so children, in our dramatic play area, would "cook" with a wok, use chop sticks, "read" a Chinese Menu, see a Chinese newspaper and/or wear Chinese children's clothing any time during the year.

Thanksgiving was the holiday I refused to perpetuate in the way it was celebrated in too many classrooms. The origin of Thanksgiving was told as a time Native Americans invited Pilgrims to sit with them and share a harvest feast—fiction. I had to find a way to enjoy this National Holiday while respecting Native Americans, American Indians.

I was delighted to work with people from the Mitchell Museum of the American Indian in Evanston, Illinois (MMAI) and after our extensive research, and conversations, I created a workshop for early childhood educators which I conducted at the Museum for many years, *Rethinking Thanksgiving: Celebrating Corn the Gift of the Indians.* I presented my workshop at National Association for the Education of Early Childhood Conferences (NAEYC) in many cities across the country. My article appeared in several publications and the actual celebration in my classroom became an important part of my curriculum. (Please see Appendix E, page 174.)

Before I finished speaking at a workshop in California, I noticed a man in a white suit with a long braid who got up and walked out. Once the Q and A part was over, he returned, walked up to me and shook my hand saying "Thank You, I felt for the first time someone understood the Thanksgiving Story." To not perpetuate the "story" about Indians and Pilgrims enjoying a feast together but rather to celebrate a Harvest Holiday was respectful and more accurate. By rethinking the story I was hopefully changing it, however the myth is still taught in too many schools to too many children today.

I hung tall corn stalks in our room to begin talking about Corn, and its importance. Children removed the kernels (the seeds) which were planted and its green shoots we fed to our animals. The cracked corn became food for wild birds. Children experienced the importance of this food, the gift of the Indians in many ways as we celebrated Corn.

For our Thanksgiving celebration, families brought in foods that contained corn or corn products and we had a corn feast the week of Thanksgiving. Children made corn husk dolls, and played games that were favorites of Native American children. (Please see Appendix F, page 179.)

Our school held a yearly Halloween Parade for the lower grades. Children and teachers came dressed in costumes and families lined the parade route to cheer them on. For my very young children, those who chose to dress up were asked to wear their costumes over their clothes and bring a bag so when the parade ended they could take their costumes off and have the rest of the day unencumbered by them. Masks weren't accepted, it was my class rule—too scary.

For the years when I occupied a corner room at Lab, my little children sat on the floor outside our door and watched the parade pass by. Older children wore masks and some were scary and had to be talked about so no one was frightened on this goofy day. I was a Jack-o'-lantern one year (orange shirt with black triangle eyes nose and funny mouth pasted on it), another year I was one of our Zebra Finches—the children loved guessing my costume.

Children helped mix "Witches Brew" for our Halloween party—three juices mixed together with a few drops of red and green vegetable coloring made it a muddy, disgusting looking liquid. With added grapes, along with and a few small plastic well-washed little skeletons it became a fitting punch. Children helped create it, but were still unsure of its color and the funny "eyeballs" that sunk to the bottom of their cups. (Ah—here was yet another place for Piaget's Conservation Theory to show itself.)

Earlier I described how children rearranged their mailboxes using the alphabet, giving each child a mailbox with an address. The exposure to addresses, stamps and mailing grew. The involvement began in full after a walk to the corner mailbox to mail a letter from the class, to the class. When it was delivered to our room the children's conversations were filled with excited comments and questions. Since our school was within walking distance from the Museum of Science and Industry, I made plans to visit their Post Office Exhibit. (Unfortunately it has completely changed today.) Back in the '80s children were able to follow the route of a letter mailed at a corner mailbox in one city, transported by truck, taken to a post office for sorting, shipped by train, truck or plane, until, in its final journey it was delivered by a postal carrier to the street address on the envelope. Figuring out that stamps paid for the costs of mailing was a big discovery. The whole mail journey was too complicated for some children, but some of it was possibly understood by a few. The exhibit provided a visual, simplified version of how our country's post office system works.

Everyone in our class had multiple opportunities to put letters in correct boxes or into the "Dead Letter" box if one of the three needed items—name, address and stamp—was missing. Our mail carrier (a better name than mailman) delivered pictures or letters according to the address, a one child job most days, but the amount of mail grew tremendously around Valentine's Day. It was a process for the sender to put a name, a mailbox address, and a stamp on every valentine before it was put in the mail bag for delivery. (Our art area stored and made available many pages of stamps that families saved for us from magazines or advertisements) The number of Valentines for delivery required more than the usual one "Mail carrier" to deliver the volume of envelopes.

I shared this experience by writing "It's in the Mail." My submitted article was edited and abbreviated when it appeared in *The Instructor Magazine*, February 1989. (Please see Appendix G, page 181.) I hardly recognized it as I'd written about exposing children to alphabetical ordering and creating addresses based on a grid. I wrote the article to demonstrate that numbers become more than rote expressions as children used them in significant, meaningful, real situations. An unknown editor re-wrote my words and what a learning experience that was for me. For other manuscripts I submitted to be published I was adamant that the content not be significantly altered by an editor and it never again happened.

We celebrated Valentine's Day with cards and with a simple party to which we invited families, the children's little sibs, parents, grandparents and nannies. Our pink punch (mixed juices) was delicious served with the cookies families brought. Six names were pulled from the entire group of names in our party bag and those families were asked to bring the treats—more than enough goodies for everyone, just right amount to not overeat. Once a family name was chosen, we removed their name card from the bag—turns needed to be fair for kids and for adults.

Families celebrated Christmas, Hanukkah, Kwanza, all or none of the above, but I always presented a holiday gift to each child, delightful inexpensive or free things to give. Starting in the fall or late summer, my family collected wishbones from every chicken dinner we and our friends ate and by December the collected dried little bones (coated with colorless nail polish) were transformed into a strange necklace gift for each child. It was just perfect when fastened to a bright colored ribbon and lovingly tied on each child. The sentiment I expressed was that the bone was to be kept whole waiting to break it for a very important or special wish. By spring some of the children still wore their necklaces.

Once I collected old keys, and made each into a necklace, the explanation that went with that gift was that someday a child might find the door that opened with the key, but it could take years.

The Resource Center had wonderful little boxes, colored paper I made into packets, and odd things that I turned into satisfying gifts for the holidays.

Ground Hog Day called for another special celebration. Some years I read a story by Crockett Johnson (no longer in print) that was fun, and was of course fiction.

> When a plastic flower fell from a truck and stuck in the ground was spotted by a groundhog it appeared to be growing out of the snow. This little animal was convinced that spring must be on its way.

This great story we loved, but when I didn't have the book, and it was my favorite, I'd talk about the long name Punxsutawney, children loved saying, and we'd go outside to look for shadows. Sometimes I'd bring a copy of a February 2nd newspaper weather page to let children know if the shadow was seen or not, and if there would be six more weeks of winter.

Earth Day celebrations turned out to be different each year. (We didn't repeat the tragic return of fish to Botany Pond after the year they all died as the water was too cold). A very special celebration occurred when a parent gave us 16 tiny tree saplings for children to plant on school grounds we designated as a Nursery School Grove. Unfortunately only a very few survived. (In 2013 the area was under construction for an expansive addition and our grove would have been cut down) Some years we made lists of how we cared for the earth. It was important to celebrate Earth Day, but to care for the Earth everyday was our goal. Children picked up trash to keep our environment clean, recycled juice cans, reused paper scraps, washed cups rather than use paper ones, and the worms in our compost bin made rich soil for growing plants.

For Mozart's birthday children sang his alphabet song; we frosted graham crackers for a treat, and listened to some of the music written by this great composer when he was just a boy.

We invited a young Irish dancer, a former kindergarten student, to join us making a St. Patrick's Day celebration special. When ten year old Sheilah finished her dance many children tried keeping their arms at their sides while their feet moved quickly to the music we played. Juice served at that party was colored green of course. (We made use of vegetable coloring in so many places. What a useful thing to have on hand).

All of the celebrations, varied as they were, involved learning, a pleasant time and eating. For Charles, whose religion did not allow him to celebrate, other arrangements that respected his family's wishes were made when necessary. I always kept in mind individual children may need individual circumstances—one size does not fit all.

Children and Circumstances

Changes in our room came about for a variety of reasons. Before five year old Richard was scheduled to have surgery there were many ways we could help prepare this little boy. Setting our dramatic play to be a hospital was my first thought. Without know just how it would play out, I shared some picture books about children going to the hospital which led to wonderful comments and important questions. (Several of these titles are in the Bibliography.) Richard was quiet, but one child talked about a friend who broke his arm and from the conversations it sounded as though the arm broke off. Ah, an opening for me so I had children feel the hard parts under their skin, their bones, and I explained the word "broke" meant there was a crack in a bone, covered by skin not broken off. (Many times children's words are taken literally and need short sometimes long explanations and I made sure to give them.)

With the help of many children, we transformed our dramatic play space. All the needed props from my stored box were examined and laid out: stethoscopes, photos of hospital rooms, x-rays to hang in the window, doctor's coats donated from medical families (the sleeves cut to size so little arms would be comfortable) pencils and clipboards, syringes minus their needles and of course, bandages, many bandages. Our reason to visit the hospital came about when

I explained a doll had a broken arm that should be cared for at the hospital.

I was fortunate that a doctor parent made arrangements for our class to visit the x-ray section at the University Hospital, and the casting area. The plan was to take the doll we pretended had a broken limb and the x-ray department and the casting technician were ready for our visit.

When we arrived In the radiation department I was permitted to lie on the x-ray table, and the technician moved the huge camera back and forth over me while my children watched as it "took pictures" of the bones under my skin. The technician explained this was a different kind of camera called an x-ray machine. When I got off the table, the doll we had carried with us was next to be x-rayed.

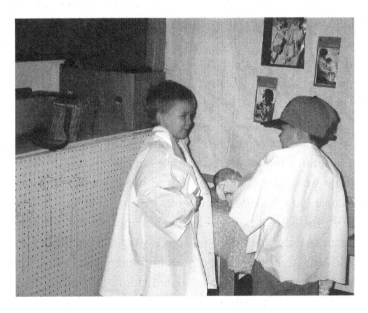

From there we walked to the casting room where children looked at x-ray films and the technician explained that a bone with a line or a crack on it showed it was broken. She proceeded to wrap the doll's arm in colored plaster gauze that soon hardened and became a cast.

We made arrangements to return within two weeks to have the cast removed. After all, dolls heal quickly!

Our second hospital trip was equally important. The well cared for doll was to have his cast removed. The saw made a shrill, loud sound when it cut through the plaster and several of the children looked frightened. The technician carefully explained and even demonstrated that this special tool, a cast saw, only cuts through plaster and stops before it reaches skin. Another very important lesson!

With the doll in a child's arms, on this second visit, we were invited to go to a floor in the children's wing. There were no ill patients in the section so we were able to visit a hospital room furnished with a bed that could be raised and lowered. (This was important and meaningful preparation for Richard's impending hospitalization.) There was a chair where an adult could comfortably sit, and space to put in a bed so an adult could sleep in the room should a child patient need to stay overnight. Just watching the empty bed go up and down wasn't satisfying. Three children volunteered to lie together on the bed while the position of their heads and feet were changed. Everyone joined in and sang—"Three in the bed and the little one said, roll over—and they all rolled over and one fell out."

What a successful visit! The doll's arm was healed, and children had the opportunity to both see and be in a hospital room. I had no way of knowing how many children would face a broken limb or a hospitalization, and I hoped these experiences might prove to be helpful.

For many children, the play that followed in our class room "hospital" was important; however Richard, whose own hospitalization was pending, did not venture into the space. He often observed others' play, but from a safe distance.

Richard was absent for ten days during which time I visited him at the hospital and brought the cards children had "written" and drawn for him. He told me about his bed and how it really did go up and down, just like when our class visited the hospital. When he returned to school, still not very strong, he became a "doctor" and added his experiences to the play, working as a doctor, but now in control of the situation.

Several years later I received a phone call at home from Lonnie's Mother. Her four year old had ridden her bicycle into some thorn bushes which severely cut her face and hands. On the way to the emergency room her very anxious Mother tried to be calm while explaining they were going to the hospital when Lonnie interrupted and said, "I know all about the hospitable Mom, remember I've been there before with Mrs. N."

A visiting professor came to the University with his family for a year and his little daughter was enrolled in my class. That same year, the President of Chile was scheduled to visit the University and after numerous phone calls I was able to make arrangements for our class to meet the motorcade. Paz, my Chilean student's Mother hand-made small national flags for each of the children to wave as they greeted the President. University Security roped the entry to the building, but because of my earlier phoning, children were permitted to sit on the short outside wall and await his car. When his long limo stopped, and the door was opened, the Chilean President saw the children waving their Chilean flags he walked directly over to them, past the crowd of press people, past the President of the University, and said "Gracias" and bowed. When Paz spoke to him in Spanish, her native language, he bent down and hugged her. The cameras rolled, and the delighted children were part of an historical moment. Whatever happened to the local newspaper picture of that day I have no idea. Sorry.

Not all the ideas or experiences came from me. The year my assistant teacher had a super suggestions, and we followed through with it children better understood Mr. Oswaldo Morales's home in Mexico. He told stories about his village and excited everyone when he suggested children could build a village like the one where he lived as a boy with its very special market. Under his wise leadership our room was transformed. The block area cabinets were rearranged to make room for some colorful carpets which covered part of the floor—the room felt electrified as he showed photographs, and illustrations of the houses, the flowers, even the brick streets. He talked about the weather in Mexico, and our village was started.

A mural committee created a colorful background drawing for the market which was taped across the wall. Other children created separate areas to define the market stalls with large unit blocks. Spaces were set up to sell real foods: baked bananas, tacos and juices, but not on the rug areas. We enlisted parents to help children with the food preparations.

Another small group created Mexican coins and bills, copied from the real ones Mr. M. shared. Children set up a cash box to receive pesos and give change. Some stalls had shoes and clothing which were not really for sale so that selling was pretend. Magazines and even newspapers were for purchasing.

Our room became a Mexican market and our Latino families helped by bringing some of their own articles to enhance the scene— enameled candle sticks, copper pots and other items—not for sale.

Invitations were hand delivered to the other kindergarten classes along with envelopes containing child made pesos for each visiting child to spend. Classes were scheduled, one at a time, so children could shop, eat, dance to the wonderful music, and listen to stories that a Mexican daddy, dressed in a serape shawl read to the small groups gathered round him.

The environment was truly Mexican and the involvement and learning went on for days. The job of the stall workers involved keeping their areas clean and tidy and appealing for their "customers".

Mr. Morales loved our new environment, as did all of us. Our Market involved everyone—children, parents, other teachers and other classes. And the wonderful smells brought one of the school engineers who followed his nose into our Market and asked if he needed pesos to buy a taco.

With a different group of youngsters, a few years after our Mexican Market experience Mr. Samer Ali was my assistant teacher. He read a special book over and over: *The Day of Ahmid's Secret* by Anne Perry Heide, and it became a favorite. Inspired by the illustrations and the story, Mr. Ali and I thought we might create the Nile River in our block area and create a market place in Egypt where he had grown up. To do this we wanted to recreate the sounds and smells, and atmosphere, so everyone got to work. The room was transformed as we cooked fava beans, turned up the volume of Egyptian music, moved some of the cabinets. We borrowed simple shawls and scarves made from colorful fabrics for children to wear. Using illustrations found in *National Geographic* magazines gave our artists ideas for creating a delightful background mural. Drawing Egyptian money, learning the names of the coins and the bills involved art, math, and social studies. But it was the book about the secret Ahmid shared, which was the best part of the experience. In the story, a little Egyptian boy learned how to write his name in Arabic. Mr. Ali wrote each of the children's names in that beautiful different way and all of us learned about a faraway country and some of its inhabitants.

Once the Cairo Market was open, children from other classes visited, shopped using Egyptian coins and bills, and ate the wonderful foods.

The only objection to our market came from the school custodian who was rather upset when he saw a blue painted "Nile River" on the floor. We had first created the river out of crumpled blue paper, but painting the floor was less slippery and more like an actual river. Even offering him some of the food didn't make him less upset. Children and teachers attempted to scrub the floor when the market had lost its usefulness, but we were not too successful. Trying to remove the river turned out to be a very messy, but a fun thing to do. Eventually our floor came clean, but it took many scrubbings.

New Needs, New Problem-solving

For me, being a teacher required observing, listening, sometimes following a gut feeling and then acting on it. If I had been asked how I would intervene, what I would do, in the following situations I couldn't have responded. The overall feeling of what needed to be done came from paying close attention to children and reacting to what seemed to be their underlying needs. The insights I had gained from my graduate studies at the Institute of Psychoanalysis in the '70s and from my work at the Gesell Institute certainly were frequently taped and in these situations my gut feeling also came into play.

I knew age could never be the exclusive criterion for advancing or retaining a child in my class. I was keenly aware of the importance of not rushing a child before he was ready, of providing developmental time. My special training urged me to look closely at the little boy I felt required "A Gift of Time", as taught by Dr. Arnold Gesell, at the Institute in New Haven, Connecticut I had been privileged to attend.

Neils was a tall boy who chose to create block structures, to climb, to run, but he struggled to put the letters of his name on paper, to cut with a scissors, to participate in putting together a simple puzzle if it had ten or more pieces. His attention span was brief, but he was not disruptive or in any way a difficult child to have in a class. Although he was a Kindergartener when I taught a Nursery/Kindergarten two year group, he most often chose to play, to seek out, the Nursery younger children. A red flag went up for me. What would happen to him next in a first grade room?

I invited Neils' parents to observe him as he interacted in the classroom, and we met to discuss what they saw, and what the first grade expectations would be for him. We explored possibly providing extra time, another Kindergarten year, before sending him on to first grade. They too saw Neils as less ready than his Kindergarten classmates, and together we decided to give him time to grow and develop. His Father was afraid if Neils did not move on to first grade, he would see this as a failure. I needed time to be alone with this boy to pave the way for his having another Kindergarten year and suggested they invite me to their home (several blocks from school) so Neils and I could walk there together, giving us talking time. They agreed with the plan, and I was invited to lunch.

As we walked, holding hands, I began our conversation by asking what he thought we might be eating and he said maybe chicken soup and bologna sandwiches. In no time, maybe after just one block of our walk, I learned that he didn't like bologna last year, but now it was his favorite. Here was my opening, I talked about how I had noticed that he didn't like writing, I talked about how I had noticed that he didn't like making letters or rhymes with words, the stuff kids do a lot of in first grade, Maybe it was just like bologna, he needed time to decide these things were really neat. We walked along in silence for a block more before I told him that his parents and I thought he might like to have more time in school for building and playing, things he loved, and though other kids were ready for first grade, he seemed to need more play time. I asked how he felt about that, and without a moment's hesitation, his answer was "Good".

We walked on another block before we arrived at his house. Lunch conversation was a talkative time, but no one brought up next year's school placement. The year ended without having a clear picture of keeping him in Kindergarten or moving him on with his classmates. During the summer, his mother called to tell me she knew Neils felt another year of Kindergarten was right for him. At the community swimming pool she had overheard him telling another boy that he was going to be in Kindergarten for the next year, 'cause he wasn't ready for first grade yet.

Neil's parents and I were certain the plan would be successful because he felt it was right for him. Providing an extra year isn't always the solution for every questionable child, but in this case, it was just right. Because our school had three other kindergarten classes, Neils began his second Kindergarten year with a different teacher down the hall. As I watched him from a distance, kept in touch with his teacher, I was convinced the decision did give him "The Gift of Time."

There were other children and their families that required extra time and thought, but I've chosen to explain one child in particular, a great example of the importance of standing up for a child even against the administration's pressure.

Ben had been asked to leave two nursery schools, and was only accepted in my kindergarten class after I'd received a call from his therapist and together we thought my room would be a good placement for him. I literally and figuratively fought to have him in my class knowing he would exhibit behavioral and social problems. I was able to offer him a space and insist he be accepted because I fortunately had two assistant teachers and could provide individual attention when needed—an essential consideration.

He began school, and for a few days seemed to pose no difficulties, however his behavior soon changed. Ben was unable to keep focused for any length of time; took toys from the hands of other children; shouted out his thoughts at rug time, sometimes yelled and even screamed, the reason being unclear to me. But he also had wonderful moments that were calm and settled. He could think through difficult situations, and I saw him as a bright child.

I often sat with him on my lap, containing him after an upset until he was calm, and though he did take a large portion of time, I and the children could see his growth. Classmates would say, "Nice going Ben, you can have these blocks now that you asked." "Hey Ben, thanks for giving me back the book, I wasn't finished with it yet."

Our school prided itself on having a diverse population and to me diversity could not be based on race alone. The response of Ben's classmates convinced me children were learning ways to help a child in need.

One day Ethel's Mother came to the classroom door just as children were entering. She insisted on talking to me, "Right Now." I asked her to please return later as I did not want to take time from children for any parents, but she wasn't to be stopped and so began her harangue. She insisted I transfer Ben to another class. She continued saying she was paying for her daughter's education, (Lab is an Independent School charging tuition), and did not want Ben, a disruptive child to be in the same classroom. My response was that Ben would not be moved as he was slowly feeling acceptance, and was showing signs of progress. Children, including Ethel, were learning how to help him. If she wanted, she could certainly ask to have her Ethel moved to another room.

For sure, I could never have stood up to her had I been a new, inexperienced teacher, but I wasn't. I made eye contact, I listened, something I learned from my first teaching experience and I then pointed out the positives for Ethel being a member of my class: she was having a good year as evidenced by the fact that she was more assertive, more vocal, showing interest in all parts of the program, and enjoying several friends. Her mother said nothing more. Though she did not have her moved to another room, her anger at me persisted.

I would not budge from my stand of not transferring Ben to another room because I felt strongly that he could grow in an accepting environment. All of us could see his behaviors slowly change. Without ever discussing it or pointing it out, I felt that children were aware should their behavior ever be out of control, gentle help would be provided for them too. I thought it very important for children to learn to accept different behaviors and by so doing begin to be empathetic. Day by day it was happening, Ben was slowly showing modest gains in control and children were aware of this growth.

The year with Ben was my last before I retired. Ethel's Mother never said "Good-bye" nor did she attend any of the marvelous retirement parties given by parents and faculty. At our closing classroom party Ethel's mother did not speak to me. On the last morning she picked up Ethel and hurried her off. My attitude, after struggling with it for a long time was you never win them all. But this story didn't end with my retirement.

An extraordinary happening took place twelve years after Ben had moved on to 1st grade in another school here in the community and later to a school in a suburb. I was standing in an empty room having just finished presenting my workshop for Teachers in Louisville, Kentucky when a woman walked into and stood in front of me. With a question in her voice said, "You're Mrs. Needlman, aren't you?" She then introduced herself as Ben's grandmother and after a hug she told me she wanted to thank me for being so involved and caring in Ben's early life. He was now a seventeen year old with spiked hair and "the works" (whatever that meant), a bright student and doing fine academically and socially. She explained she saw a flyer about the workshop with my name and since she now lived in Louisville, she had to find me and thank me for being there for Ben. What better gift could I have as a teacher?

I've so many stories of individual help I selected this next story whose outcome I had no idea would be successful. When Greta seemed to be confused, needed to make a decision, was tired, this four and a half year old little girl popped her finger in her mouth, gazed into the distance and appeared to have disappeared from the world. One day, while she was seated close to me, I'd just finished reading a story, I asked Greta how she felt about sucking her thumb in school. "I don't like it, some kids call me a baby, but I don't know when I do it. It happens." I asked if she'd like me to help by reminding her when I saw her finger sucking? She nodded a strong "YES". I might tap her shoulder gently whenever I was near and then it would be her decision to keep sucking or stop. And when we were farther away from each other, I'd just tap my shoulder and if she saw me, she would know what to do. She said she would promise to stop. I quickly said that I knew this was a promise easily broken—so I told Greta I'd done the same thing when I was a little girl—I'd sucked my thumb, I'd promised to stop and I never could keep that promise and breaking a promise made me feel terrible. Rather than promise, I suggested we work together to help her remember—when I saw her thumb in her mouth I'd tap her on her shoulder, and she could continue or stop sucking. She could decide.

Some days I tapped her shoulder three or more times, or I'd catch her eye and tap my shoulder if she wasn't in reach. Over the course of several week of shoulder tapping, and smiling, Greta limited her thumb sucking to rest time and by the end of the school year, she no longer needed it. It was our private thing and it seemed to work for her (Maybe it was my help, but most likely it meant she was ready to give it up on her own.) Things I'll never know. This was a hunch I had, no real reason to believe it would help, but worth trying.

And now I'll share a few other children's stories that required extra thought and time on my part. A very active little boy, years later diagnosed with ADD, could not sit for a rug time, or become productively engaged in any area of the room without first using up his excess energy. I, or an assistant teacher, would each day invite this child and any others interested to put on their coats, if the weather warranted it, and go out for a jog in the courtyard. It was never for a race. Each child only ran to increase his/her record— once around on Monday, so on Tuesday perhaps it would be one and a half jogs around the yard. After a jog time which took maybe five minutes or less, the rest of the day for this active child settled down to constructive involvements and he was comfortable and manageable—great for me, for the rest of the class and certainly for him.

As I revisited these days of a child with ADD, (Attention Deficit Disorder) not yet clearly defined in the late '70's by psychologists I found support, and caring, along with the physical activity, was a positive means of early intervention. I still have contact with him, now a college graduate holding down an important job, and my adult friend.

The importance of not just listening to a child, but really hearing the message behind the words or the actions is best understood by sharing the following vignette. Chris's parents separated soon after his birth and Father was unavailable to this little boy. Chris had little or perhaps no recollection of him. Surprisingly, Father contacted Chris's Mother's and he now, three years later, wanted to become part of his son's life. It was the Dad's idea that they might bond if the two of them went camping. To be in contact with his Father was both exciting and somewhat strange for this little boy. On Monday, Chris and his Mom told me about the plans. The camping trip was to take place over a weekend yet to be determined. Chris and his Dad were going to sleep in a tent in the woods.

On Tuesday Chris complained of a terrible stomach ache and using the toilet gave no relief. He said his stomach was really hurting on Wednesday and Thursday as well, and this seemed to be time for the two of us to have a private conversation. I invited him to sit down at the little table placed in a corner of the hallway, next to the classroom—a special place I set up for informal kid-teacher conferences and story dictation. A well-used table.

I asked Chris what going camping meant, and what he thought would happen when he and his Dad went off together on their adventure. He looked me right in the eyes and told me that big animals could come into a tent in the night, and it would be really dangerous and scary. I listened, and while still holding our eye contact, with my arm around his shoulder, I told him that I camp with my own kids often, the ones who call me Mom, and the only animals we ever see are little squirrels, and sometimes rabbits if we are lucky. I knew that his Dad would be sure to take extra good care of him. They might cook their food outside, take walks, play ball, and maybe sing around a campfire before they climbed into a cozy tent to cuddle and talk and go to sleep. The expression on his face changed, he looked less tense, almost relaxed. I asked how his stomach felt, and he looked surprised. "Oh, it's good." That ended the worry and his bodily response to his tensions and fears.

For this child it was so important I was able to expose his concerns and help him sort them through. I had recognized his tiny subtle clues that meant help was needed and by listening to his worries I did something constructive to actually provide that help. Today I volunteer alongside Chris's Mother at the Zoo garden, and one morning Chris, home for a week, came to meet me. We hugged and this six foot three inch man and I so enjoyed reminiscing during our all to brief meeting—no mention of the camping incident, just a big thanks for that great year in my room long ago.

My next vignette is about a child with juvenile diabetes. Having him in my class required careful interactions so I could be prepared to do whatever was necessary. Barry and his Mother would stop at my Science Corner from the time he was a two year old when he and his Mother brought his older sister to her classroom. He would pull his pacifier out of his mouth and ask important questions about the displays or the hands-on materials at my Science Center. He called me "Man"; Needlman was too much for him to say. I loved his questions, his interesting ideas and I wanted to know this boy and be his teacher. As it happened, I waited to retire until we spent a year of Kindergarten together.

I met with both his parents before the opening of the school year to gain information in preparation for knowing how to best meet his needs. I wanted to learn about regulating his food intake, any special timing or activity restrictions and his parents supplied me with clear, insightful information.

Once the school year began, it was this little guy who explained to the children that his pancreas didn't work right so he had to have special food at special times. Barry's mother came every day before lunch to prick his finger and check his sugar level while they were both seated at our little table just outside our door in the hall. He always invited other kids to see what his Mom did to keep him healthy. What an attitude! What wonderful support from his parents!

His food requirements were quite different from the other children—for example, he needed to have 15 saltine crackers when they were the snacks food; when we went on a trip it was important that food was available at a specific time. I changed the scheduled time for my children to have their physical education class so that it didn't interfere with the time Barry required food, and the PE teacher was more than willing to accommodate. Whenever there was to be a birthday celebration, I'd inform his Mother ahead of time and she would take fruit or something from his lunch box so that he could have a cupcake without its frosting or half a brownie at party time. If the treat was not one Barry could eat, his Mother brought him an acceptable treat from home he would enjoy, and made certain that an extra box of his treats were kept in the classroom cabinet for any unplanned times.

I learned so much from working with Barry and his parents that I was able to co-author with my son, Dr. Robert Needlman "Dealing with Diabetes" for Scholastic's *Early Childhood Today*. This was one of the many important topics under the title, "The Doctor and His Mom" published monthly between 1994 and 2000. (Please see Appendix H, page 183.)

Parent Participation

The diverse backgrounds, the unusual interesting practices, the ethnic celebrations of the families represented in my classroom led me to invite an adult from each family to sign up and volunteer one Friday in the year to come and share with the children anything unique to their family be it a tradition, a holiday, a religious practice, foods, or maybe a story from their own childhood. It was on these Fridays that the children were exposed to and gained an understanding of the similarities and the differences of each family and of each child.

One of the most unusual Friday presentations was that given by a mother who was a midwife. She brought a baby doll, and a plastic pelvis that she introduced, and with gentle, wonderful explanations, she "delivered a baby." The classroom walls could have collapsed and not one child would have noticed. My reading of this was that the mystery of birth was no longer a puzzle that a young child could not grasp, but a wonderful experience that was meaningful to each child.

An angered parent came to our room the following morning enraged that I had not told her ahead of time what her child was to be exposed to childbirth. I've no idea what this child said about the experience to her parents. My response was that I had expected families to trust my sensitivity when it came to curriculum experiences, and that I would never check with parents before giving children information that was factual and age appropriate. She had nothing more to say and walked out of the door. Oh well, all in a day's work.

On another Friday, a Thai mother took out of a beautiful cloth bag a small pitcher and bowl which she filled with warm water. I kneeled down on a beautiful little rug and each child poured a few drops from the pitcher onto my hands to wish me a long healthy life. As children waited their turn the room was almost silent, and the importance of this beautiful ceremony seemed to be understood. It was certainly a wonderful experience for all of us, but most important to Mia, the little Thai girl.

This particular story is about a student from a biracial family, Marcy, her father, Caucasian, her mother, African American. Their family spent holidays and family times with both maternal and paternal families and Dr. and Mrs. M. were involved members of a group of biracial families. They both worked hard to successfully raise Marcy and her younger brother to be very accepting of their family composition – black and white.

One afternoon Dr. M. stormed into the classroom stating he had to talk to me immediately. As we walked out into the hallway he began saying that his Marcy had come home and told her mother she didn't want anything to do with anyone who was black, and he needed to know what had taken place at school. I was somewhat taken aback, but instead of being defensive or attempting to answer his outburst suggested that both of us take time to think it over and meet again the next afternoon when we could sit down and carefully talk through this very alarming situation. He agreed.

The day Dr. M and I were to meet, Marcy, in the dramatic play area, dressed in long silk scarves and wearing high heels was asked by her playmates if she was a white princess, and she said "No" I am a black princess, because you know I'm both and I can be whatever I want to be."

That very afternoon I began the conversation with Dr. M. saying I imagined that from the time he had first become a husband and then a father he feared such an occurrence and now I wondered if he wasn't possibly overreacting. Before he had time to respond I related the incident of the morning. As we talked, sipping coffee at a little table in the quiet room, now relaxed, he said he was thrilled to hear Marcy's words to her friends, and recognized that as parents, they had absolutely done lots of right things to help their child be comfortable and accepting of their family. There was no question for either of us; their biracial parenting was certainly successful.

During Marcy's second year in my Nursery/ Kindergarten classroom her mother was having a very difficult pregnancy and was bedridden for much of it. She was hospitalized in her eighth month to save the pregnancy and Marcy's Dad was very concerned that his little daughter was really missing her Mom. I invited Daddy to drop Marcy off at my house early in the morning giving him time to visit his wife. We, Marcy and I, had breakfast in my kitchen and walked to school together. I took her home with me at the end of the school day and we baked and played in the afternoon until her Daddy came to pick her up even though their housekeeper was home with her younger brother. Within the week, the hospital put a mattress on the floor and Marcy was able to stay overnight in her Mom's room. Between these hospital stays and our time together everyone weathered those last weeks before Marcy's new baby brother was born.

In those bedridden days, before the hospitalization, Mrs. M. had a small refrigerator placed near her bed so she could be somewhat self-sufficient when alone. After the birth of their son, she donated the refrigerator to our classroom. It was this little refrigerator which was well used and it remained in my room for many years. (It was in the tiny freezer space we kept the dead birds that now are part of the Nature Museum's collection.) My original acceptance of the refrigerator was that it would be on loan until Marcy or one of her brothers needed it years later in their college dorm room. (I fortunately became the teacher for Marcy's sibs) The refrigerator ended up at Washington University in St. Louis the year I retired.

My husband and I attended a college graduation party for Marcy, and our friendship continues to this day. Becoming involved in the lives of children and their families I found to be so important, and I loved it.

Maybe I was a busy body teacher since I'll never exactly know if it was it my observing, my intuition, or my concern for a child whose home situation was very sad, but somehow I understood Arthur needed extra help, and here's his story.

Just six months prior to Arthur's entry into my Nursery classroom, his father died after a long, difficult cancer that had required many hospitalizations. The first weeks of school there were no particularly outstanding situations for this little boy and his adjustment to the classroom, to the other children was fairly typical for a three and a half year old child. One day at lunchtime I heard him quietly sobbing, unable to eat his food or be consoled. Try as I might, his tears continued and his sobs turned to strong cries. I rethought his mornings and realized that I had never seen him enter our classroom bathroom. Was it his toilet needs that were the cause of his discomfort and upset? Was he afraid of our toilets or unable to take care of his personal needs? When I thought I knew, I sat with him on my lap and told him it would be just fine with me if he didn't want to use the toilet in our room, he could just use his pants. He looked surprised at first, then shocked and said, in a very tiny voice that his housekeeper would be mad if he brought home dirty underpants. (I knew his mother was not home until late each day and it was the housekeeper who might well react just as he thought.)

I told Arthur I had a washing machine at my house, we had clean underpants at school that would make him comfortable. This would be our secret. On that very day I watched Arthur move to a corner of the room, concentrate and then look around for me. Together we cleaned and changed him and I took the soiled clothing home to my washing machine. This scenario took place only for a short period before his widowed mother, now stronger and functioning much better, said she was taking Arthur and his five-year old sister to Disneyland for a little holiday they all needed. On their return, Arthur hurried to whisper in my ear that he had learned to use the toilet, and didn't need my help anymore. Lunch time tears totally stopped, and he happily went into the small bathroom during mornings.

The years passed and I watched this little family grow and change. Because the Laboratory Schools housed Nursery through 12th grade, as Arthur moved on through the school we often met in the hallways or he would stop by my classroom to say "Hi". He sometimes moved close to give me a hug and then looked somewhat embarrassed. Neither of us ever discussed our "secret" and now, many, many years later, he is a college graduate. I still receive phone calls or holiday cards from him yearly. I'm certain he has long forgotten just what our secret was, but he knew that I had played a now forgotten role in his life.

Human Rights in My Early Childhood Classroom

As my students came from many different backgrounds I decided to share the huge topic of Human Rights with them. Teachers and schools were concerned with diversity in the '70, but once I located an adaptation for children about the Universal Declaration of Human Rights, I was ready to make Human Rights understandable as I thought it so much more inclusive.

I introduced Universal Human Rights by first asking children what Universal meant. Peter said, "That's easy—you know it's everything, the Universe". And so we began our many conversations and experiences based on the rights of all human beings. We talked about the things the children in our room needed, not what they wanted, but really needed. I wrote down their words.

- Someone to kiss you goodnight
- Food to eat
- A warm bed
- Toys
- A school to go to

The list contained many more "needs" it also contained their "wants". Children had to figure out the difference between the two words. I explained there were "rights" or "needs" that every person no matter who or where they lived must have.

A long time ago people thought about these rights and put them down in a special document that we'd be talking about, and these people from different places with different kinds of ideas, and schools and living in different kinds of weather and in different kinds of homes wrote something they named the *Universal Declaration of Human Rights*. Of course the word Declaration, needed to be defined and that discussion was amazing. I brought out a small book, *The Universal Declaration of Human Rights: an Adaptation for Children* by Ruth Rocha and Octavio Roth. Over the following weeks I read only a few pages of the UDHR at any one time and every page I read evoked a great deal of conversation as we talked about what the pictures and the words meant. Children expressed surprise as they recognized their own needs, their rights were written about on the pages in this simplified version of the Declaration made by the United Nations in 1948.

Over many weeks we talked about the UDHR, and some children used inventive spelling to write what seemed most important to them. There were children not ready to write words and in their place they drew pictures. Here are some samples that led me to feel children understood "Rights", but of course, I could never be certain this was so. I have kept their drawings and writings and used them when I presented workshops "Human Rights Belongs in Early Childhood Classrooms" at conferences across the country.

AVREBO KAN B FRE

(EVERYBODY CAN BE FREE)

U KAN NOT TL PEPL HO TO MARE

(YOU CANNOT TELL PEOPLE WHO TO MARRY)

NO MR WRAZ

(NO MORE WARS)

It was decided that we'd create a doll, the same age as the children in the room, who would come from somewhere in the "Universe" but not our country. Two long sheets of paper were laid on the floor and several children roughly traced the outline of the child who volunteered to be the model. With adult help the "doll" was cut out and the two sheets stapled together, leaving an open space to stuff crumpled sheets of newspaper between the front and back. We repeated the way that the Big Friendly Giant was made, the one described earlier. The larger than life child was a little girl, a four or a five year old. The next step was to determine where in the world this little girl lived. A child spun our globe and when the spinning stopped, another of the children touched a spot which turned out to be India. Our child was from India. Out of many names suggested, the one agreed upon was Razwana, the name of a child's grandmother who came from India. The class dictated a list of the things Razwana, our Indian little girl, would need and were her rights. I wrote their words down and read the list aloud. Children were amazed—they found her "Rights" were the very same as those they required—to be kissed goodnight, to have food, a bed, and to go to school. Razwana had a prominent place in our classroom for the year, sometimes seated, sometimes lying on the floor. She became a reminder of why the Declaration was named Universal. Children everywhere have the same or very similar needs or rights.

After many conversations children created their own *Declaration of Human Rights*, and this list is representative of what they dictated:

These Rights are for Everyone.

They are "Universal." This means the whole Universe.

You need parents or grown-ups to take care of you.

All people need to be respected, even kids.

You can play with anyone you want—everyone is equal.

You have the right to go to school.

You must think for yourself.

You have the right to do any job you want when you grow up.

No one can tell you what to do in your own home.

Parents need to help children grow—It's their job to sometimes tell kids what to do

Everyone needs love.

You can have your own things.

**It doesn't matter what color your skin or hair is—
people are born equal.**

Once the classroom Declaration was written, discussed and accepted, we planned a day for a formal signing of the document which I had rewritten on a long sheet of parchment paper. I set a jar of black paint along with a quill pen, a gift from a lawyer parent, on a small table and explained that children should find some time during the day to sign their Declaration. I also explained that no one should ever sign a document unless he/she understands and believes what the document says.

All during the day, two, sometimes more children lined up patiently waiting to sign either their initials or name on their document and this Declaration remained in our room for the full school year. We often re-read it, agreeing with each line.

I pointed out the quill pen illustrated in the UDHR adaptation for children which I duplicated, and made into a bookmark for each child to take home to remember the signing of their Declaration of Human Rights.

To have written a Declaration was just the beginning of an awareness of Rights for everyone. There were frequent times that I'd ask about the Declaration or remind a child that he had put his initials on the Declaration and that meant that he believed it—it did change behaviors toward one another.

In keeping with the UDHR, we found a way to talk about slavery. While preparing some corn kernels for feeding wild birds, children hammered some kernels we covered with a thick towel and the rest of us sang about Jimmy or Suzie or Tommy whoever was having a turn cracking corn. The song named the hammering child followed by the line "and I don't care, my Master's gone away." I asked what the composer of the song meant when it spoke of a Master? We talked about slavery that then took us right to the Universal Declaration of Human Rights. No one has the right to be a master, and no one should ever be a slave.

A favorite book read repeatedly was *Follow the Drinking Gourd* (the story of the escaping slaves' impossibly difficult journey north to freedom). The children requested that I read this book again and again, and fortunately for us a fifth grade class invited our children to be the audience when they produced a play based on the book about the Drinking Gourd.

Late one evening I received a phone call from my Nigerian parent, Dr. O., who related the following episode that took place in their car during the morning ride to school. Mother and Father in the front seats were discussing problems of Human Rights violations in Nigeria when their four year old son, my little guy, said "Excuse me, but don't you think if they're having Human Rights trouble in Nigeria it's time to call Mrs. Needlman." What a grand phone call to receive!

Each year I did repeat, though with some differences, an introduction to the *Universal Declaration of Human Rights for Children*. Families learned ours was a Human Rights Classroom. The important place to begin big ideas is with little children.

After talking about skin color I put out bowls of both chocolate and cream colored pudding and children covered their hands with the one they wanted which for many changed their skin color. I questioned if the color of their hands made them now different kids with brown skin, or tan, not really white, if they needed different things and so began conversations about skin color – a subject we had talked about many other times. It was wonderful to hear that it didn't matter what color they were, they were still kids, still needing the same love and stuff as when their skin was different without the pudding. This experience was just a part of our Human Rights work that happened whenever possible in our room.

Remember our fish tank that housed several small fish from Botany Pond? Well, I added a catfish to the aquarium with the understanding that it would keep the tank clean. While some children watched, several little fish began to attack the catfish even though it was larger than they were. This was very upsetting and I was told to take the catfish out. I explained that sometimes a new fish, a stranger, one the fish hadn't know before might cause them to pick on it, but once they knew there was enough food for all, and space for each of them they could live together and get along. It took no more than two days for all of the swimming fish to be content in one tank. What a great lesson for understanding and acceptance of one that may be different. This lesson of acceptance was worth remembering and one I hadn't expected to happen when I introduced the new fish—to be sure I did talk about it with the children.

I've written about the bins that fit into a cabinet and housed the private "mailboxes" for each child. Anyone could put things into a mailbox, but only the child whose name appeared on the outside could take things out of it. Not even parents or teachers were to remove items from a child's box. Children were delighted with the idea of privacy, so a toy from home could be safely housed in a child's mailbox if the owner did not want to share it. Children learned to respect the privacy of each other. How important to have a private place! The Universal Declaration of Human Rights addressed private property, and we had a perfect example of it in the classroom.

Children had been voting for many things, for example deciding what their earned money should support—raised hands were counted, or children stood or sat to be counted, but for this next very important issues, there was another ways children could vote— by secret ballot.

At the time of a local election we talked about adults going to a polling place to mark a ballot for the person they thought should be a leader in our city, or state, or country. Children were to vote by marking a ballot, but not for a leader, but to decide on an important issue for our class – guns in our room. I did not want it to just be *my* decision, but one every member of the class participated in making. Children helped set up a voting area before we walked to the polling place in the public school one block away. Our private place was created out of two hollow blocks with a board across them facing a wall to provide privacy for each voter.

I received permission before school on election morning for our class to sit on the floor, out of the way, to watch adults register, sign in, take their ballots, and move to the small private booths to mark their ballots. The children could see only the shoes and legs of the people who voted and moved on so others could vote or cast their ballots.

Back at school I introduced the prepared ballot which was simply a small piece of paper with a square next to the word **YES,** and a square next to the **NO.** Each voter was to use the small pointed stick affixed to the Styrofoam block to punch a hole that signified her/his vote. Even four year olds could "read" the words. YES meant guns were okay. NO meant a vote for no guns. Children needed to Think For Themselves. It was acceptable to talk about how someone felt, but no one could tell another child how to vote. The voting took place throughout the day—a child picked up a ballot, registered by checking her/his name off the class list, and once the ballot was marked – one vote, one mark – it was put in a closed box made with a slit on its top. Three children volunteered to count the ballots and report the results at the end of the day.

I left myself open for whatever would happen. The children who wanted guns tried to influence others—"Guns are really good, we can keep the room safe with them"; "You gotta vote YES—we want guns."

The voting line was never too long, and by lunchtime every name had been checked. I'd already decided that if the children wanted guns, we'd let them be used for a period, and then I would, once again, begin a campaign of showing children's discomfort when there was violent play, the way I had approached the subject prior to the voting.

Everyone gathered around the committee as they sorted the ballots. Two were spoiled—both Yes and No had been punched. The others were put into two piles, and when counted, NO had 2 more ballots in its pile than YES, and it was decided, **NO GUNS IN OUR ROOM.**

I explained that I would no longer talk about guns, the children had voted, they had decided. One morning, after the voting, I did hear a child with a Lego made gun being told, "We voted on it. You can't make guns in our room." By gosh, it worked! I took a risk asking children to decide about guns – the results were great this particular year, and I must say, I didn't try it again. Why spoil a good thing?

For me Human Rights belonged in the life of my classroom and was brought up and talked about throughout the school year. On January 10, 1948, the United Nations UDHR was written, and on that same date we had a party in our classroom.

In 1988, Amnesty International published a pamphlet on teaching Human Rights in Early Childhood Classrooms, and I wrote much of the material that appeared in it. It unfortunately is no longer available except for my saved copy.

Ways to Motivate Curiosity

Whenever I thought it time to introduce some new road to travel with children, I would set out different items, books, sometimes photographs in the classroom as a way to redirect children and open new areas for learning. I placed several books about totems on a table and watched first one then a few youngsters look to see what they were about. They were drawn to the pictures and talked about what they surmised the books said, and of course, raised questions about what they "read." "What's this for?" "How come the parts are all different"? "That thing looks like a witch or maybe some other scary thing, why?" To respond, I used the name Totems and chose appropriate paragraphs, and/or captions under pictures to read aloud allowing many more children to become interested, even fascinated. It was decided, after having shared books with their photographs and drawings, that these totems must have been very large. Once the exploration began children stretched out on the floor in the hallway, head to foot until all 21 of them created a long attached line—a living totem. This was the first attempt to demonstrate just how large a totem might be. Each of the children spread their arms and/or legs or folded them and told a story, a brief totem story based on what we had read. This live totem was very impressive.

Following the initial creation of our human totem, children made individual totems from cut out papers pasted on long strips of cardboard. Continuing the exploration, children created still other totems out of play dough and clay. As in most areas of a nursery or kindergarten class, not everyone was interested, and it was never my intention to have the entire class working on any one project. The *piece-de-resistance* was when a very talented assistant teacher, Jenny G. introduced cardboard boxes of various sizes we'd been collecting. She put out only one box a day, to be decorated and to eventually become part of a totem. Children used cups cut from egg cartons glued to a box, cardboard thread cones were fastened along with feathers, and strange shaped corrugated cut pieces were affixed. On each day a different unadorned box appeared, and a face, or wings with unusual features was created from it. As a box was completed it was stored out of sight.

It was Sarah, a 5 year old who applied white paint that she insisted was really needed to make the Totem look wonderful. Wow, she was right, it looked extraordinary. On the last day of school we assembled one box on top of the other and our Totem reached the ceiling. This Totem was a one-time project for one group of children, and even though it turned out to be so successful it was never repeated.

Using the information gained from the library books we read, children dictated their "non-fiction" ideas and a Totem book was the result. The book and Totem stayed in the hallway at the Laboratory Schools for two years and when the new Chicago Harold Washington Main Public Library in downtown Chicago opened, I contacted the children's librarian, and our totem, along with its book, found a home there.

The artists and creators, by this time, were second graders. I sent a letter to each family inviting them to visit the Children's Room at the Main Library. It was tiny Elizabeth who said, as she and her Mother walked into the lovely new Library room, "Oh my God, that's my totem!"

This Totem now resides in my home and guests often mistake it for an important piece of primitive art—and they are right on two counts. It is very primitive and an important piece of art it is.

Our Totem while still in the classroom.

Our totem was created in what we referred to as the art area, and children were always welcome to move into this inviting space. It was furnished with a large table that had just enough room for six chairs for six children to work along-side each other. A cabinet with bins (much like the mailboxes) was next to the table and it was filled with both fresh papers -plain, lined, colored, cut into small or large pieces along with recycled papers of different shapes, recycled envelopes, stamps, crayons, markers, pencils, pens, scissors, small boxes, stickers, and whatever recycled materials could possibly be used by creative artists. Children were encouraged to choose whatever materials they needed for their own art projects. Very few paper scraps became garbage instead they became items for creative works the children constructed.

Of course, there were little blank books made from a single piece of paper, some small, some larger, available for our writers and illustrators.

(Please see Appendix I, page 187.)

The art area was always a busy place. A favorite job required tearing off the little pieces of paper that clung to our many broken crayon stubs in preparation for melting them in either a small can (an empty frozen juice container) or any container we happened to have. (Jar lids made great circular crayons easy to hold). Once again we had a great use for the little oven as the heat made a rainbow crayon of colors rather than the unattractive little bits and pieces. When the melting was taking place, children watched through the oven window as the many color bits melted and flowed into each other.

Three paint easels were prominently placed in my classroom and we made sure they had paper and containers of paints available to be used every day. I strongly believe having access to painting should not ever be considered as a treat, but an expectation for children to enjoy in my nursery and/or kindergarten classroom.

It was interesting to change the brushes sometimes setting out those that were small and pointy while at other times I made wide ones available. Children seemed to enjoy the different results that came from using different sized brushes. Paints were also changed— sometimes the bright primary colors changed to pastels when I mixed in white paint. A handful of sand or sawdust added to the paints created a different texture, and colored newsprint or pages from a wallpaper book made for unusual backgrounds. I created this area so children could really make their own creations.

The paints jars always held fresh paints, and the brushes were supple and ready to be used, so either before or after school I spent time in preparing the art area. How well I remember the day I added egg yolks to the tempera paint. Each brush stroke was brilliant, the yellows amazing, but after two days there was an odor in the room I was, at first, unable to identify. Finally I realized it was rancid egg. It was one of those Live and Learn ideas. I'd love to know how the old masters kept their egg based paints from rotting.

We didn't have computers when I first began teaching at Lab, but in the early '80s my room was supplied with one. The Computer Lab teacher suggested we create a class website. We talked about it and agreed each child would draw a picture of a fish that fit on a two inch by three inch piece of paper. In place of a fish head would be a photo of each child's own face. The creatively drawn fish were delightful. Once each photo was glued on its fish body and the fish cut out, they were arranged on one page which I scanned and gave to the computer teacher. Once the website was set up each child sat at a computer in the Lab to view our class contribution. It was our joke, all these little fish swimming in a school. Our swimming fish pictures remained on the Laboratory Schools website for several years—unfortunately once I retired the website disappeared. I wasn't clever enough to keep a photo of it.

Remembering the many creative things begun in the art area, children worked on this next described useful project. Families sent lunchboxes with their children every day; some very healthy and appealing, others, commercial packaged lunches. I recognized there was a way we could help, so I kept a close look at the lunch remains that ended up as compost or became food for our pets. Of course I tried to play particular notice of those lunches that were fully enjoyed by the children. After gathering my "data" as to which foods were eaten, which ended up untouched, I suggested we create a Lunchbox Ideas Book. The response was enthusiastic. The words were to be written by an adult and illustrated by children. After talking about foods children enjoyed—each child choose a lunch idea and illustrated its page. It was easy to print one recipe or idea on an index card and put all the cards together with spiral binding. Once compiled, a book went home to each family. It was simple but without the advent of duplicating machines and the binding gadget—I might have chosen to punch holes and tie each little book. Binding was easier and available. Here are a few examples of some of the entries:

- A plastic container with cream cheese, peanut butter, or sour cream for dipping snap peas, celery sticks or carrots.

- A chicken leg, and a bread and butter sandwich and a bunch of grapes made a great page.
- A small thermos with hot water kept a hot dog warm or was filled with a favorite soup.
- Bologna or a slice of ham or turkey rolled around a bread stick; Juice in a thermos.
- Some dinner leftovers tasted better heated, (remember we had an oven that was available and heated foods quickly.
- Cheese sticks, apples or bananas to smear with peanut butter were some of the most original ideas that appeared on our Lunch Box Cook Book pages.

This classroom Lunchbox Ideas Book contained environmentally sound, healthy foods and it proved to be useful for parents who were always looking for new ideas for lunches. Maybe we should have had it published, but we never did.

I wanted small juice boxes that appeared in many lunches to be replaced by thermoses which would be environmentally acceptable. Try as I might, juice boxes continued to appear. Perhaps I may have raised some awareness, back in the '80s, of not adding to waste fill.

The works of famous artists placed on walls added a great deal to our room and were frequently changed to retain interest. (Miro's work was a favorite for a time, while another time the work of Grandma Moses was voted as The Best.) The most important pictures hanging in the classroom were always those made by children. (I hung a line high off the floor and affixed art work with clothespins when we ran out of wall space.) I tried to display their work with simple colored paper frames that were perfectly acceptable and after hanging for a period of time the art work was sent to the artist's homes. I did keep the frames as they were time-consuming to construct. Paintings were rolled and marked with the artist's name and mailbox address to be delivered by the mail carrier child to the correct box.

Enjoying Clean Up, Really?

————•————

Humor and fun had an important place in our classroom. Since clean-up time is an essential part of every school day it required the help of each of its members. We made it a time for cooperative efforts. Some jobs required children becoming a living conveyor belt as they handled a load of blocks that needed to be shelved. The "workers" lined up from the block cabinet to where the blocks were scattered, and with adult help, spaced themselves close enough to each other to be able to hand a block from child to child until the last child put the block in its correct space in the block cabinet. No one was required to move, instead each child pretended to be cemented in place while the objects on the floor were passed along and the floor cleaned up in no time. We found involvement in the conveyor belt job was usually accompanied by laughter, sometimes by songs.

I was fortunate to have a jib crane in the block area, constructed by my husband, but before it could be operated safely, a child had to pass a Jib Crane test and be licensed. Each personalized license (Made on a 2" x3" card) had a space for a child's name, and the date saying the bearer of the card had successfully passed a jib crane test. It was stamped with a circular seal. (Good use for my outdated notary seal which made a raised impression on the license making it appeared quite important and official.)

Only a licensed child was allowed to use the jib crane which meant that the bag was to be carefully filled with all its contents inside—nothing sticking out of it and the area first surveyed so that other children were out of the path of the swinging crane. Because of the need for licenses, accidents did not happen—using this machine safely was a serious experience. Over time everyone became licensed. If any one of the safety rules was violated, the forgetting child's license was revoked for a day. By George, it worked! A former licensed kindergarten child as a 7th-grader stopped by the classroom to show me that he still carried his license with him, it being a bit worse for wear.

Another way that made a clean-up job interesting for youngsters was to create an inclined plane. A long board or heavy cardboard piece was placed with one end in a storage bin or container on the floor, the other end propped up on a large hollow block or a low chair. Children were encouraged to place small objects that were to be picked up on the high end of the plane and watch as they slid down into their final resting spot. Almost every child could be enticed to engage in some aspect of clean-up time making it a positive part of each day.

I've talked about our community recycling center within walking distance from our school; a wonderful resource which operated on a barter system. I frequently would drop off a few bags of recycled crushed cans, and return to school with two bags of useful items. There were always items we found uses for: printed envelopes that children used in many ways; containers wonderful for storing things in the room; out of print wallpaper books we added to the art area; to mention only a few of the many recycled items children put to good use in our classroom.

Perhaps the best item from the recycling center was a discarded huge cone, open at both ends that came from the Geophysics Department at the University, part of an actual spaceship. It was too large to fit into my car, and Ken Dunn, the genius who started this early recycling center in the '80s, delivered it in his truck to my classroom. (I could have converted a discarded appliance box into a space ship, but having this real cone was perfect.) Children became involved in space travel and explored many possible cooperative ways to play at being astronauts. Along with this playing were, of course, opportunities for learning.

The cone, turned on its side was large enough for two children to sit in side by side. Of course, before anyone went off into space she/he had to be properly attired. An astronaut could only enter once having donned a five-gallon ice cream container discarded from an ice cream shop in the neighborhood-a space helmet. It was perfect once a large area was cut out for a child's face and its exterior painted by our artists. Wonderful imaginative space play took place in this "spaceship", and researched books, of course, made up a big part of it. When the cone was no longer needed for going on space adventures, I set it upright and placed a circular strong plastic sheet, also obtained from the recycling center, on the narrower round top and it became a large table surface that housed a variety of things Children today may have less interest in space exploration than they did in my teaching days, but maybe not.

I found some of my most creative curriculum came from scanning newspapers and magazines and choosing items that might spark the interest of children. One such article was about Steve Fawcett, a very unusual millionaire who made several attempts at circumnavigating the earth in a Hot Air Balloon. The flight of the "Solo Spirit" became something that evolved into a huge involvement in my classroom. I shared the newspaper articles with my children about Mr. Fawcett's flight and they became very excited when I suggested they could create their very own hot air balloon basket.

Of course, we did research to learn the balloon or envelope was 150 feet tall. In order for children to visualize its tremendous size, we went to the large sidewalks in our courtyard and with a yard stick, children counted off 150 feet on the cement. Additional research gave us the basket size which was led to creating a facsimile of it in our classroom out of cardboard boxes cut and taped to size. It took many children working together to create our sturdy replica. The food supply of ready to eat meals was reproduced in trays (families recycled grocery plastic ones for us) which children filled with "foods" they made from clay and play-dough. Youngsters figured out the number of (empty) gallon containers for the water Mr. Fawcett would require for washing, for drinking and cooking. Kids agreed water was an essential need, and the empty bottles too were stored in the basket.

As one could imagine, a lengthy conversation took place as children discussed the toilet needs for the balloonist. Those discussions covered many aspects of life in a balloon such as where and how he would rest depending on the winds and what he would do when it rained. The project took us into all parts of the curriculum—literacy, science, math, art, geography and even music were involved. Unfortunately Mr. Fawcett's attempt was unsuccessful, but our involvement was anything but—it was a huge success.

Years after my class engaged in the balloon creation, in 2007 Mr. Fawcett disappeared while conducting yet another mission, and he was proclaimed dead after months of searching. At that time I wonder if the children who were involved in the Balloon Project when they were very young, made any connection to the news articles on Steve Fawcett with their involvement when they were in kindergarten.

Remember the piano with an octave I printed with numbers on each of its keys? I only briefly shared some of the music experiences but I must write about what started when a fourth grader (a former Nursery student) stopped for a hug on her way to music. Annie carried a small violin shaped case, and suddenly I had an idea. I asked if she'd like to give my little children a five minute concert, but she would first have to check with her teacher. She returned that afternoon and said she could come on her lunch hour, her teacher agreed to have her bring her violin to our room for a concert. Annie was our first musician, and soon, with the help of the music teacher we had a variety of instrumentalists providing not only recognition of their instruments, but explanations of the need to practice.

At each concert my children, the musician's audience, first had to name the instrument sometimes while still in its case which was not always an easy task. We were privileged to have several violinists clarinetists, cellists and flutists come, but the one most difficult to imagine was a singer. Her instrument was her voice and not one child was able to guess how she made music. The pianist also posed a challenge. How special for nursery/kindergarten children to know when they were fourth graders and beginning musicians, they would be invited to present a five minute concert. The audience was quiet, showed their appreciation by clapping and even singing Twinkle, Twinkle a piece that many of the musicians performed.

Winding Down the Year

I shared my stories about what I did to make the beginning of the school year comfortable—easy separations, sending post cards, a tan bark spreading party, waiting for shelves to fill once the children's needs were known. The ending of the year was also very important. Several weeks prior to the last day of school I set in motion things to help make the year's closing comfortable, knowing change is tough for little children, and for me too.

Closure began during a group time as children dictated their favorite happenings of the year and so began the Remembering Lists—the best stories, the field trips, the games, the music, the concerts, the holiday celebrations, and so much more that seemed memorable. The list grew as more special happenings were recalled. When I was ready to duplicate the lists, there were enough items to make up a Remembering Booklet for each child to take home on the very last day of the semester.

I think the most environmentally valuable part of the ending of school happened when I requested several cartons of rolls of 100 paper cups be delivered to our room. Together we calculated every 2 days 100 cups or one roll would have been used for snacks and lunches had children not washed our reusable cups. Children counted every 2 numbers on the number line, (the one we had kept from day one) and removed a 100 cup roll from the box. (We had done this same counting mid-year count and created a huge pile that represented cups saved.) As the year was coming to an end, the size of the mound of unused rolls heaped on the rug was very impressive. Ours was clearly an environmentally aware classroom. We never did figure out how many trees our washing plastic cups had saved, but the counting and the heap of cup rolls was fun and a great math experience. It was one way to see that our classroom was ending for the year.

Whatever children's artwork was hanging on our walls was carefully removed, rolled up, and the artist's name and mailbox address was put on the roll for the mail carriers to deliver to the "mail boxes." The walls of the room were bare, but with each final step, everyone was being prepared for what was to come next—summer vacation, a new class in the fall, or for some, returning to this very same room, but change was clearly happening.

I shared a wonderful book by Morris Philipson; *Everything Changes All of the Time.* It was the perfect book to read, and I did so most years except when the author's son was my student. This little boy told me, in no uncertain terms, that right in the book it said. "This book is for Alex" so I could not read it to other children. I respected his wishes. That year we just talked about how things change.

Children helped by washing and then closing up bins of toys, scrubbing hollow blocks in the water table, wrapping the cabinets in paper, rolling up the rugs to be sent to be cleaned, drawing on the notes to families to make arrangements to care for some of our animals. Families were involved as well by washing and returning clean painting aprons and even window curtains ready to be stored for the next year. All in all the tone of the room was transformed for those last days. It became a different open space.

One year we turned the space ship, the one from the recycling center, on end and filled it with discarded tennis balls—there were at least sixty or more of them. I'd printed each child's name on one of them and the children climbed on a hollow block, a make-shift step, and two children at a time giggled as they stood in amongst the tennis balls, falling over while searching for their named ball. Great fun!

We drew hopscotch patterns on the floor with chalk, made "feet paintings" (barefoot toes dipped in paint) rather than finger ones, and re-read favorite stories, and poems. It was the time to celebrate the birthdays that would take place over the summer, and committees planned the refreshments for our final, last day party. Because everyone was involved in these constructive days, the good-byes seemed to be comfortable for just about everyone.

I had watched the teacher in the next room continue day after day wearing a breathing apparatus and being short of temper with her classes. She had been a wonderful teacher, but she remained in the profession too long, and was now ill, but continued to teach. I overheard third graders when they thought I was out of earshot, "playing school" I knew the teacher they were pretending to be though she was nameless in their play. They took on stern looks, and acted with a shortness of temper. It was by this teacher's example that I knew I would leave teaching before I no longer was loved, or loved what I was doing. I always knew it would be important to recognize when my time to retire approached.

My love of teaching hadn't changed, but one afternoon when I was reading aloud to my kindergarten class of children comfortably lying on their spread out blankets on the floor, listening to every word. I lost my focus and the words on the page seemed to be sliding into each other. Before I realized it, I had fallen asleep. I believe it was only for a few moments, and when I shook my head and was again awake, a little voice said, "Mrs. Needlman, you were sleeping." No one woke me because it was an established fact: if anyone falls asleep, never disturb her/him. Once fully awake I told the children, "The reason I need to retire at the end of this school year is that I really need a nap in the afternoon."

Afterword

During my teaching years, I'm proud to say, I received several awards: The Kohl/McCormick Outstanding Teacher Award; a letter of recommendation from the United States Secretary of Education, Richard Riley; a certificate of acknowledgement for outstanding leadership and dedication by the Independent Schools Association of the Central States, along with commendation from the Golden Apple Foundation for excellence in Teaching. But the award I most cherish came from my granddaughter when she was a second grader.

TFK PEACE PRIZE
Presented to GLORIA NEEDLMAN
By GRACE NEEDLMAN
You are a peacemaker because
You are a great person and a great gramma.
You also teach peace to everyone you come across.

John Dewey wrote, "To find out what one is fitted to do, and to secure an opportunity to do it, is the key to happiness." I found my chosen profession, teaching young children, and I was fortunate to be able to spend my professional life in John Dewey's School, the University of Chicago Laboratory Schools.

Appendices

Appendix A:

Make Holes In The Environment
And Let Children See Inside

by Gloria Needlman[1]

After numerous phone calls to the university purchasing department to convince the buyer that I had good reason for ordering transparent plastic "P" trap pipes for my classroom at the University of Chicago Nursery School, it finally put the purchase order through. The pipes were to be used as part of my program to uncover and expose some of the mysteries children find in their daily lives and to allow 3- and 4-year-olds to see inside wherever possible and safe. Knowing that most of the knowledge a child gains is obtained by observing, gathering information, making inferences, measuring and classifying, I wanted my classroom to be a place where the environment helped children learn about their physical world.

Some of my plans were hampered by building codes and university regulations. A lucite panel designed to replace a wall would have made visible the wiring conduit from the floor outlet to the light switch. Unfortunately, it was prohibited by the fire code. The obstacles were many, but my nursery school classroom eventually had see-through pipes under the bathroom sinks, a toilet tank that exposed the work of the lever, and a piano that let children see what happens when the keys are pressed and the pedals moved.

When planning a new classroom, or remodeling an old one, preschool center directors and teachers might suggest that some

---

[1] From *Children Today*, U.S. Department of Public Health, November-December 1981. Used with permission.

construction be purposefully left exposed. Other techniques discussed here can also add to the richness of any preschool environment. The low sinks in a school bathroom are in constant use. Children wash paint brushes, clean sandy cars and trucks, fill bowls with water for pet animals, rinse soapy sponges—and occasionally wash hands. Often objects slide through the drain, and sometimes they are carefully placed there. Every nursery school teacher can attest to the problems created by overflowing water, clogged sinks and stopped-up pipes. What preventive measures might be taken to lessen the incidents of newspaper piles on the floor to soak up floods? How best to cut down on calls to the plumber when a plunger isn't successful? (Plunging is an activity that fascinates children. It still goes on in our school, but now it is usually just an experience, not a necessity.)

I thought that clear pipes installed under each sink might help prevent some of these problems. Being able to see them might interest children in what happens to the water, the paint and the sand as they are rinsed off objects. Would children be interested in seeing what happened? Would they even notice? Would they observe? I had to know.

The plastic pipes were eventually installed under our sinks. The colored water that flowed from paint brushes and ran through the pipes became a source of great interest. The children worked in teams. Some washed, some watched. We seldom had to dislodge small objects from inside the drain. Children began to take a real interest in books about water, and *Let's Look Under the City*[2] became a favorite for children to read to themselves, or to have read to them. (I kept a copy on the windowsill in the bathroom.) The children's curiosity about what happened to the water prompted us to trace the pipes through the building to the basement and out to the sewer down the street.

---

[2] *Let's Look Under the City* by Herman and Nina Schneider, illustrated by the Halls, New York, William R. Scott, Inc., 1958.

I also removed the top of the water closet, allowing the children to observe the working of the flushing lever. It was difficult, though, for small children to see the water and the action at the bottom of the tank. What was needed was a transparent panel in front, so children could observe the machinery to find out how it worked. This was the start of a long correspondence with a plumbing fixture manufacturer, who could perhaps furnish me with such plumbing equipment.

My needs and desires interested a buyer in the company and he shipped a demonstration toilet and tank to the university nursery school. It was ready to be installed, but it never happened. The tank, though exactly what I had wanted—with a lucite panel in the front—was part of a 2-piece unit, and the bowl and tank in my classroom were in one piece. The bowl on the new unit was cut in half with lucite on the cut side. It may have been useful as a demonstration model, but hardly functional for a school. Friendly campus plumbers assured me that they could locate a 2-piece toilet and install my "see-through tank." I'm still waiting! The equipment is now in storage, and this phase of "How Things Work" remains incomplete.

A repairman's busy schedule helped me identify another possible learning project. A leaking radiator pipe on the third floor of the school necessitated ripping a section of the floor boards for access to the pipe. It took several weeks before carpenters were able to repair the floor, once the pipes were fixed. During that time, children and teachers were privileged to see through the floor and into the space where the pipes and wiring lie.

On the third floor, we could see into the space that exists between our floor and the ceiling of the floor below. It wasn't until after the carpenters had replaced the floor boards and the tile men had begun to lay the tiles that I realized that a Lucite piece, put in place of the wood flooring, would have allowed us to see permanently this inside part of the building. It could have remained exposed and yet been safer than the open space we had so enjoyed. Perhaps others might have the foresight to install a visible panel, or portion of one, for viewing the insides of their buildings. Here, then, we would have a mystery that observing children could solve: is the floor really the ceiling for downstairs?

An old upright piano has become another "See how it works" site in our school. The piano had been made with a removable panel in front, exposing the strings and hammers and also the pedals and their mechanism. I removed the panels and created a place for children to sit and observe the action of hammers, strings and pedals. A picture sign was hung near the piano to remind children to keep their hands away, for the good of the piano and for the safety of small fingers. The exposed piano became one for both eyes and ears to enjoy. Children respected the rules set and many a child watched as another child, a parent or a teacher created music with the keys.

Construction companies have recognized the interest adults display when a hole in the ground is made by earth-moving equipment; they provide peepholes for viewers. We might learn from them and provide the same sort of stimulation "holes"—throughout many aspects of the environment—for preschoolers. Such an environment helps answer the unasked questions, "How was it made?" and "How does it work?" Planned holes in the classroom environment can become learning tools for children.

Gloria Needlman, on leave as a head teacher from the University of Chicago Laboratory Schools, is conducting science programs for young children and their parents at the Museum of Science and Industry in Chicago.

Appendix B:

Raise Birds to Raise Questions

By Gloria Needlman[3]

During the years I taught nursery school and third grade at the University of Chicago Laboratory Schools, I kept an aviary in a quiet corner of my classroom. The cage contained watering tubes, seed cups, fresh-cut branches, a bath dish, two nesting baskets, and a pair of zebra finches. On first look the colorful little birds might have appeared to be nothing more than bright decorations; but my reasons for having them in my classroom went far beyond their aesthetic value.

Birds do all sorts of things that raise all sorts of questions. They chirp, fly, bathe, preen, eat, build nests, lay and hatch eggs, and do myriad other things people rarely have the privilege to witness firsthand. Having them in my classroom provided a scientific laboratory that afforded opportunities for children to observe, to contemplate, to make inferences, to classify information, as well as to develop new interests and challenges. When children have their curiosities aroused, I have found, they become eager and capable learners. What better reason, then, to raise birds in the classroom?

I was fortunate to have been given a fully equipped cage, but bird cages are not difficult to construct. You can make one simply by tacking wire or nylon mesh to a wooden frame (36 by 18 by 38 inches is a good size) with a removable tray. A pet shop can tell you how to equip it, or suggest a book that can. When I purchased my first male and female finches, I made arrangements with the shop

---

[3] Reprinted by permission from *Learning*® magazine February 1982. Copyright 1982, The Education Center, LLC. All rights reserved.

to return the birds at the end of the school year, along with any fledglings they might produce, thus alleviating the problems of care over the summer and of inbreeding. The shop agreed to issue a credit slip that I could use the following fall to purchase a new pair. One year the breeding was so spectacular, three clutches were hatched, and by selling the young birds, I was able to repay my initial investment. (Few curriculum projects are as financially self sustaining.)

Each fall I began with an empty cage, and the children and I would talk about the birds that would soon come to live in it. Together we read books about finches, and planned ahead for their care. We located Australia, which is where zebra finches originated, on a world map. After an introductory period that varied from group to group, I brought the birds to school. I always chose a Friday to present them, because it assured the birds of a quiet weekend to adjust to their new surroundings, and created an air of excitement among the children, who looked forward to Monday to get acquainted with the new arrivals.

It didn't take long for the birds to adapt to their new environment. The children, too, quickly became accustomed to the bird sounds while retaining an active curiosity in the birds. During quiet moments of the day, a child could always be found sitting on the rug near the cage, watching the birds bathe, sleep or eat. In my pre-school classes, we noted the similarities and differences of our birds and the various pets the children had at home: dogs, fish, guinea pigs, etc. When the children began to be aware of the birds outside, we compared birds in captivity with birds in the wild. We set out food to feed the winter birds—a hungry sparrow or, if we were lucky, a cardinal.

The children watched with eager anticipation as our finches started building a nest with the bits of torn tissue, shredded burlap and dried grasses we had placed on the floor of their cage. Both the male and the female showed great perseverance as they struggled to create a nest inside one or both of the nesting baskets. More and more information was required by my children to explain what they were observing. Their questions were direct, and so, as much as possible, were my answers. Sometimes I had to answer, "I don't know, but let's find out". or, "No one seems to know, but perhaps by watching we'll be able to find the answer." Always I encouraged questions, and listened carefully to the children's retelling of the information they had taken in.

Our study of finches sent us into all subject areas. My third graders read and wrote about birds. They created an ongoing bulletin board display with up-to-date notices about our finches' development in the nesting, egg laying and hatching processes. They wrote letters to neighboring classes inviting them to come see the birds, at which time my students would regale their guests with everything they had learned about birds in general and zebra finches in particular.

Following our map work of Australia, we studied the climate, vegetation and other bird populations of the continent. This led to interest in bird species in our own area, and later, in the spring, to weekly before-school bird-watching expeditions to a nearby park. (Parents were invited to join these expeditions, which in some cases kindled a new and possibly lifelong family hobby.)

The first discovery of eggs in our aviary was always an electrifying moment. We kept a careful check of the calendar to note the gestation period (usually 10 to 12 days). Sometimes the eggs failed to hatch, and the children were quick to ask why. "Perhaps they weren't fertilized," I'd suggest, using the word both with my preschool children and with the older ones. (Everyone loves a big new word.) After explaining fertilization in simple terms, I would open one of the eggs to find out why it hadn't hatched. Sometimes we would discover the familiar egg white and yolk, which meant the egg was unfertilized. This often led my third graders to a lengthy discussion about breeding and mating among birds, and sometimes about human mating. (An interesting fact about finches is that they choose mates for life.)

Once we opened an egg that had remained unhatched for several weeks and found a dead embryo in side. We talked about stillbirths and about the possible reasons for the chick's death, and then about death itself. My preschool and third grade students were fascinated by the dead bird, and by the topic of death.

Happily, there were many occasions on which the eggs did hatch. For weeks the children watched faithfully the growth of the feathers on the chicks' tiny bodies and the way both the mother and father fed their young (by dropping into the chick's beaks food they had first digested and then regurgitated). The question "Are they boys or girls?" was always asked, but the sex of young birds cannot be accurately determined. Birds have internal sex organs, and their sex is identifiable solely by their feather coloring. Newly hatched chicks have no feathers; it takes five or six weeks for their first feathers to grow, and colors appear only after the first molting.

Each aspect of bird development eventually became related to human development, and specifically to each child's own growth and behavior. For example, the young birds had a particular call that we learned to recognize. It seemed to mean "Feed me," for that was how the parents responded. Often a fledgling that was capable of feeding itself from the seed dish would call out "Feed me" when it saw one of its parents. This behavior was comparable to that of a preschooler who, despite being capable of performing some task, calls for adult assistance.

Raising birds in the classroom is not without its hardships. I had to go to school during the holidays to care for them, and to drive long distances to purchase fresh finch seed and millet spray. Once a week I had to stay after school to thoroughly clean the cage. The project requires a great deal of patience in answering the endless questions students raise about all phases of bird (and by extension, human) development. But if providing interest-rousing, thought-provoking, firsthand experiences to promote children's learning is a goal of your teaching, then by all means, consider raising birds.

Resources

Foreign Birds for Beginners by D.H.S. Risdon (London Iliffe Books, 1965).

Introduction to Finches and Softbills by Hank Bates and Bob Busenbark (T.F.H. Publications, 1970).

How Babies Are Made by Andrew C. Andry and Steven Schepp (Time-Life Books, 1968).

Gloria Needlman is a teacher at the University of Chicago Laboratory Schools. She spent last year on a leave of absence to write and develop a preschool science program at the Museum of Science and Industry in Chicago, Ill.

Appendix C:

Seeds of Preschool Science[4]

By Gloria Needlman

It all started, quite by chance, in our school play yard. The opening week of school, the yard was a painful place for children to play. Plants with tiny stickers had grown at the base of the slide and around much of the other playground equipment. Rather than wait for the custodial crew to remove them, we decided to tackle them ourselves.

It took seven days and five trash bags to complete the job. Following each weeding session, we would return to the classroom covered with stickers. In the process of carefully removing them from our clothes, shoes and skin, we began to look closely at the villainous, porcupinelike hitchhikers. Questions began to emerge from children and teachers alike. What were these prickly devils? And what purpose did they serve?

To try to find answers to these questions, we cut into some of the stickers. What we discovered—that the prickly things were actually coverings for tiny seeds—set off another round of questions and launched a primary science investigation that would continue throughout the year.

Collection and Comparison

An awareness of seeds in our environment carried quickly from the play yard to the lunch table. Soon the children were collecting and comparing the seeds they discovered in their dessert fruits. As the children ate, they talked about what they saw, and they began to classify: some seeds are round, some pointed; some are smooth, others have rough skins. Almost every day the lunch table became a place of seed discovery.

I sent home notes to parents requesting that they send to school any seeds they found in the fruits and vegetables they ate. It wasn't long before the children were bringing in seeds of all sizes, shapes and colors. We looked at them with naked eyes and through magnifying glasses. The children arranged them by size, from the tiny green pepper seed to the mango seed, the largest we had. They sorted them by color and shape, then displayed them by gluing them onto pieces of wood.

We placed some of the seeds in small Ziploc bags with identification labels, and stapled the bags to a bulletin board. As these seeds began to germinate, we transferred them to dirt-filled flower pots. Quite by accident, and to our amazement, several corn kernels sprouted in our moist sand table as well as in the dirt.

An unusual gourd was brought to school. It had already dried, and its seeds rattled when the children shook it. The gourd had a paper-thin covering. When the children peeled it, a dried, stringy pulp was uncovered.

What we had was a loofa sponge, the kind sold at bath shops and cosmetic counters. After removing the outer skin, we collected the small round black seeds inside, then took turns scrubbing our hands with the dried sponge material. The children thus made another discovery: the coverings of some seeds are fruits, but some protective coverings are useful in other ways.

Observation and Research

On walks around the community we collected seeds: winged ones from the maple, prickly balls from the chestnut, and acorns from the mighty oak. When the milkweed pods we found in a vacant lot ripened, we selected a windy day to free the seeds. As the umbrella chutes floated across the play yard, the children discovered another way that seeds get distributed: they float in the wind.

Sometimes our seed study took us to the school library, where we conducted research to find out about a particular seed. One such research task was initiated when Daniel found five little round brown seeds on his walk to school. "They came from a tree," Daniel told us. He knew nothing else about them.

Our research began in the reference section of the library. In a tree guide we found a picture of seeds similar to those in Daniel's hand, but not exactly the same. To find the true name of the seed, we needed more information, so I asked Daniel to bring in a leaf from the tree.

The following morning, Daniel brought in several leaves with seeds hanging from the underside. With this additional information, the identification process proceeded. The children looked at the leaves, then at each picture in the book, responding yes or no to each picture. Whenever there was a yes response, I asked what aspect of the leaves was the same: was it size, shape, color? The research was completed successfully when the class found a picture of a linden tree, showing seeds and leaves that clearly matched what Daniel held in his hand. The children were thrilled, as was I. To identify one seed was important, but to know that information is contained in books, that plants can be named, that libraries are places to find specific information—this knowledge was of even greater importance to these young learners.

We not only collected and studied seeds, we cooked and ate many. The pumpkin seeds from our jack-o' lantern made delicious eating when we baked and salted them. We picked popcorn plants, stalks and all, dried the corn on the cob, then removed the kernels for popping. It was quite a discovery for the children to learn that the kernels on the cob are the seeds of the plant. We gathered the seeds from dried wildflowers, and the children used them for collage work at the art table. The pods from the honey locust became percussion instruments that made gentle sounds when struck with the side of the hand. Other pods were opened and their smooth brown seeds collected for counting games.

Of course, not every child became involved in every aspect of seed discovery. Some children showed more interest than others, some participated in more activities, but each child was involved in at least a portion of the project. There was no special time of the day devoted to the study of seeds. Whenever an interest was noted, whenever an observation involving seeds occurred, we talked, we classified and, if possible, we identified. Through this approach, we discovered the true seeds of primary science.

Gloria Needlman is a teacher at the University of Chicago Laboratory Nursery School.

Appendix D:

Matters of Life and Death in a Classroom[5]

By Gloria Needlman

The discovery of a mass of apparently dead worms leads a class of young children to explore—with their teacher's aid and comfort—their concepts and feelings about life and death.

The subjects of death and life were never planned as a curriculum unit for my young students. Nonetheless, they occupied an important part of our school year as they grew naturally out of a series of school experiences.

Our first exposure to death came in an unexpected manner. One cool, cloudy October afternoon, some of the children and I had gone to the play yard and found that the morning rain had left huge puddles at the base of the slide and in other low areas. The adjacent play area looked more attractive, so the children ran through the gate onto the clay surface.

"Hey, look, dead worms!" yelled Brian, as he squatted down to examine the tiny brown things lying on the ground. A few children glanced in Brian's direction, seemed to agree with him that these were dead worms and hurried off to continue investigating. Sara, who had joined Brian, picked up a dead worm in her gloved fingers to examine it more closely. Then, from various parts of the play area, other children shouted, "I found one." "Here's lots more of them." "I gots three."

I heard the children's words and sensed something behind them. Certainly there was excitement in their discovery but also some

---

hesitation and perhaps even fear. I realized that there were some real concerns underlying their excitement, but I could only guess what those concerns might be. I needed to know more.

"How do you know the worms are dead?" I asked, hoping to hold their interest.

The children looked closer at the still worms. "I just know they're dead," one boy offered simply. One of the girls said she found a dead worm in her backyard one day, and it looked just like these worms. One boy responded, "It looks dead, so it is." And still another stated emphatically, "That's how it is. It's dead." The children seemed to agree that the worms were dead, but I was interested to know what they meant by the term.

I picked up a worm and said that I did not know if the worm was truly dead. I only knew for sure that it wasn't moving. I explained that I would try to warm it in my hand, to see if it might be still merely because it was cold. The children huddled close to see what the worm would do in my hand. I covered the worm gently with my fingers, and for a few seconds there was absolute silence.

When I opened my fingers, the small creature moved. Immediately there was a flurry of comments. "It's un dead!" "It was only sleeping." "The worm got alive again."

Within a few moments, I heard a range of young children's ideas about death: death is like sleep; things can come alive after death; whatever moves is "undead." A single question and one little worm had opened the way for the children to talk about death and to explore the subjects of life and death in a situation that was not fraught with heavy emotions.

Clarification Through Investigation

As a teacher, I have learned to listen not only to the spoken words of children, but to their unspoken curiosities and queries as well. My class's discovery, made while playing outside, had elicited all kinds of clues as to the children's conceptions-and misconceptions-about death. It was time to go a step further and provide them with the materials and experiences they needed to investigate the subject more deeply.

When we were ready to go indoors, the children collected as many cold "dead" worms as they could carry. Some children shrank away from touching worms. I encouraged these youngsters to participate by watching others, and suggested that as each child became less fearful, he or she might be ready to hold a worm. But I stressed that it was perfectly acceptable for some children to merely watch. Once inside, we placed the worms on a table. We immediately attracted the attention of the children and teachers who had remained indoors when my young discoverers explained that they had found dead worms, and that some had "got alive 'cause they got warmed up." One child quickly corrected: "The dead ones didn't really get alive; they were that way." Clearly there was some confusion about what had occurred on the play yard. To clarify things, I asked another question. "How will you know which of these worms is dead and which is alive?"

Again, there were many responses, but everyone seemed to agree with one little girl's hypothesis: "If the worms don't move, even a bit, even when they're inside on the table, that means they're dead. Really dead."

I repeated the idea and asked the children if they thought it was true that when something cannot move by itself, even a tiny bit, ever again, it can be labeled "dead." This idea seemed acceptable to everyone.

Following this discussion, I asked the children to sort the worms on the table into two groups-those believed dead and those thought to be alive. I provided magnifying glasses so that the children could examine the worms more closely. We decided that the live worms would live in our terrarium. We carefully printed a sign, clipped it to a clothespin and stuck it in the dirt. It read Worms Live Here. The children carefully placed the live worms in their new habitat, watching as they burrowed into the soil.

We decided that the dead worms should be returned outdoors. As the children carried the worms out, some of them described the way the dead worms looked and felt: *unmoving, wrinkly, hard, funny-looking, squishy.*

Some children mentioned pets of their own that had died. One child told how his mother's grandmother had been dead for a really long time, while Bill, whose grandfather had died only recently, listened quietly. One girl told about how she cried when her dog died. These young children were coming to terms with death from both a physical and emotional perspective.

Someone said, "I won't ever die," and immediately several others chimed in, "Me neither." One girl responded, "My daddy says things can't live always, so everything dies sometime." Each child was given the opportunity to express her or his concerns, thoughts and fears in a supportive, nonemotional setting. Every response was respected. And there were repeated assurances that most people live long, long lives.

Building Blocks to Understanding

The dead worms were the beginning of many experiences over the school year in which the children grew to recognize death as part of the natural cycle of life. There was always time for discussion, whenever and wherever it seemed needed.

Several weeks after the worm incident, a small fish floated to the top of our aquarium, and there was a loud announcement proclaiming that the fish was dead. Some children wanted to touch it, so we scooped it out and many hands held the tiny, stiff fish. One of the children said it was dead because it didn't move. "It can't swim anymore and that means it's dead." One child thought it was sad that the fish had died; another wanted to know why it had died. We talked about the many possible reasons for its death. Perhaps the water temperature was too low; maybe the fish had needed more food, or maybe it had been overfed; possibly it had been very sick. Since we didn't know how old the fish was, it was possible it had died of old age. The safe environment of the classroom allowed the children to make conjectures as well as express their personal feelings about the dead fish.

During each encounter with death and the discussion that followed it, I attended to the unspoken questions of the children: "Will my mommy die?" "Who will care for me if my parents die?" In an effort to address these neverstated fears, I would always mention that most people live to be quite old, and that when someone close to us dies, there is always another loving adult to help us and care for us. Invariably, upon making these assertions, I would notice the children's faces become more relaxed.

We used each experience with death as a building block toward an understanding of life and death. I purposely repeated some information as well as added new knowledge to help reassure the children and aid in their understanding. Each experience, each discussion, therefore helped my young children to make some sense of the matters of life and death.

Gloria Needlman teaches kindergarten at the University of Chicago Laboratory Schools.

Appendix E:

Rethinking Thanksgiving[6]

Editor's Note: Chicago AEYC asked two members to address the issue of Rethinking Thanksgiving. Below are their responses, proceeded by some rationale for the necessity for evaluating "traditional" celebrations in the classroom. A related article on page 6 offers some insights into the process of "rethinking."

Historical Background

by Gloria Needlman

During November schools across the United States prepare to celebrate the National Holiday THANKSGIVING, and many early childhood teachers make available Pilgrim hats and collars, along with headbands and feathers important to teaching about the first Thanksgiving in 1621. But, in 1992 teachers must. be aware that this day is not looked upon as a day of celebration by all Americans, not by the Natives of this land. Our educational focus needs to be redirected, the energies of classrooms moved toward a celebration which is more acceptable to and more respectful of Native Americans.

The history we have passed to generations of children relates the Pilgrims fled oppression to achieve religious freedoms in a new land and after a difficult voyage arrived in Plymouth to build their lives anew. Their skills for living in this new environment were few,

---

[6] From *Chicago AEYC Connections*, a publication of the Chicago Metropolitan Association for the Education of Young Children, Volume One, Number One, October-November 1992. Used with permission.

and the help they received from the indigenous people, referred to as Indians, allowed them to survive. Soon after their arrival they began to settle the land lived on by a small number of Pawtuxet Indians—their numbers being greatly reduced by plague introduced by English explorers before the Pilgrims landed. The nearest other people were the Wampanoag whose lands stretched from present day Narragansett Bay to Cape Cod. They were farmers and hunters, and they too had met Europeans before the arrival of the Pilgrims. The Wampanoag were the people to have celebrated the bountiful harvest with the handful of Pilgrims who survived. The Wampanoag had long been thankful for their harvest and had held their own celebration upon which was fashioned the "first" Thanksgiving.

It must be remembered that history is written by the "winners" and the tragedy of the Native People has been minimized leaving the stereotypes: "uncivilized," simple people with an undeveloped language who, when they attempted to protect their land, were referred to as savages. Seldom do teachers relay the history which states before the European arrived the Indian Nations were developed; their spoken language complex; their beliefs, though different, were strong. What has become a day of celebration is for many descendants of the Wampanoag and other Indian Nations, a day of mourning because their way of life was destroyed, their sacred lands taken, their people sold in Europe as slaves, or left dead from disease introduced by Europeans.

What about celebrating Thanksgiving? What must schools do to change the disservice to the Indian nations we have so long perpetrated? How do we develop a curriculum that broadens children's awareness and appreciation of human experience, rather than perpetuating history as seen through Anglo-centric eyes?

Perspective One

Celebrate The "A Maizing" Plant Corn

by Gloria Needlman

One possibility as we commemorate the harvest and the thankful aspects of this holiday is to draw on and celebrate an enormous contribution to the world made by Native Americans, THE PLANT CORN. A comprehensive curriculum can be developed around this theme, focusing the more universal elements of gratitude, recognition of the human dependence on nature, and appreciation of the work of those who cultivate the land.

This "A Maizing" plant has been traced back 7,500 years—developed by indigenous peoples of the Americas. Drawings of corn have been found, tiny ears dug up at excavations in North America which are over 5,000 years old. We know the plant was hybridized by trial and error. If left to reseed itself, it would have died in a few generations. It had to be cultivated, its outer husk stripped away and its seeds removed from the cob to be sown. It became a sacred plant for those living in desert lands, or where there was rich moist soil. For many Indian nations, corn has been and is food for survival; it has an important place at the time of birth, throughout life, and as part of the ceremony at the time of death. As food it is mashed, dried, ground, rolled, baked; its stalks used for fuel, parts of the plants provide material used for shelters, it remains sacred and its harvest a special occasion.

To celebrate corn in the classroom, and then to prepare a Thanksgiving feast or snack using foods made from corn, seems a respectful way to recognize a contribution to the world which came from those who first lived and planted these lands, the Native Americans.

Corn is Maize, the Gift of the Indians, written and illustrated by Aliki is accurate, informative, and read as resource for its information, age appropriate for early childhood classrooms. But reading about corn is not enough; it should be integrated into all aspects of the curriculum—whole language, science, math, art social studies, music, physical activities, along with human rights.

In the fall take a drive to a farm and any farmer, when told that a corn plant is needed to share with city children, will give you one, roots and all, along with a bag of dried feed corn. Decorate your classroom with the tall plant, keep the ears to utilize in projects as you introduce the plant introduced by Native Americans, to your children.

Study the finger like roots that hold the tall plant erect even during tremendous winds. Have children become corn plants, dramatize growing and swaying in the winds. (First the kernels the seeds, need to be removed from the cob, planted in the earth, and with sun and rain in a short period of time changes from a tiny new sprout to a plant taller than any adult.)

Collect all the products you and the children can locate made from corn—popcorn, corn starch, corn oil, margarine, chips, cereals, to mention but a few. Set up a corn museum, or a corn table. Have children invent books about corn using pictures drawn from the packaging of the products, creating their own words, drawings. Add words to the vocabulary-germinate, soil, roots ...

Kernels, easily removed from the cob can be planted in a large pot, or unused aquarium filled with soil. After planting children can water, and observe the growing process (corn germinates in a matter of days). Feed the small plants to any vegetarian classroom pets, i.e. bunnies, guinea pigs. Hammer some kernels carefully (wrapped in a towel for safety) and sing about "Suzanne cracks corn and I don't care", and feed the cracked corn to birds during the winter. Mix corn with water to make a most delightful tactile substance—when in motion the molecules adhere to each other and it becomes a solid, left alone, it becomes a liquid. Prepare a cooked play dough and make pudding from scratch using corn starch. Grind, or hammer corn until it becomes meal to use for corn bread, (add commercial cornmeal to the recipe).

Children can make simple corn husk dolls.* According to an Iroquois Legend these dolls never have faces because once a vain corn doll so admired and bragged of her own beauty the 'Maker of All Things' removed her features as it is wrong for any one person to hold herself better than others, and the doll's work was to go and make Earth Mother's children happy, humble and content. (Corn husks can be purchased from ethnic food shops, or saved from sweet corn).

Be creative as you integrate your classroom learn around the Native American plant CORN. At your Thanksgiving celebration share a simple Navajo saying:

Hogooneh, So Be It!
There shall be happiness before us (arms stretched in front)
There shall be happiness behind us (arms stretched behind body)
There shall be happiness above us (arms stretched above head)
There shall be happiness below us (bend and touch the floor with arms)
There shall be happiness all around us (turn around with arms spread out)

Appendix F:

Directions for Corn Husk Dolls

PATTERN FOR CORN HUSK DOLLS

You will need:
* Cornhusks can be bought a fruit and vegetable stores. The bags are usually of one standard size, 2 bags should provide plenty husks for thirty students.
* 1 ball of string or 4-5 containers dental floss
* scissors
* bucket of water
* newspaper
* small amount of masking tape

Preparation:
Separate pieces of cornhusk and place them in bucket with warm water.
Soak about two hours or until soft and flexible
Cover tables with newspapers, secure with masking tape.

Instructions:
Each child should be given four pieces of cornhusk and each piece will be used for the following.
  1. Head
  2. Arms
  3. Shoulders and body
  4. Strips for tying different parts and shaping the head
1. The Head. Tear off a small piece from the fourth husk and roll husk over the ball to form the head.

piece below the neck and between the two pieces of husk extending from the head. Tie off wrists with twine and trim the edges.

3. The Shoulders. Split the third piece of husk in half and fold each half in half. Drape the halves over the upper arms to form the shoulders.

4. The Waist and Legs. Take a strip of the fourth piece of husk and tie off the waist, then trim off the bottom. This makes a doll with a dress. If you want to make a doll with legs simply divide the bottom in half to form the legs and tie off at the ankles using twine.

5. Children can leave their dolls without a face. Hair can be made of corn silk and glued to the head.

Suggestions: For young children: Pieces of husk as well as other natural materials such as twigs, bark and sand can be glued to paper to make pictures

Appendix G:

it's in the mail[7]

Set up a classroom post office just in time for Valentine's Day. Besides learning about how a post office is run, children will reinforce their letter recognition skills and learn about alphabetical order, too. About a week or two before the heartfelt holiday, arrange storage bins (or shoe boxes, old cardboard boxes, etc.) in rows on a shelf. Have each child choose a box and paste a tag with his or her first name on it. Arrange boxes in alphabetical order. Come up with a number system so that every child will have one number that will be his or her very own "address."

Have students ask at home if they can bring in used envelopes for the class to examine. Bring the lines across the stamps to their attention and introduce the word cancelled. Explain that a letter needs an unused stamp to be mailed. Cancelled lines tell us that the stamps have been used. Each envelope needs a name, address and a stamp in order to be mailed.

Set up a sorting table. Label small boxes with the letters of the alphabet representing each child's first name. On the day before Valentine's Day, have children address and stamp their cards in class. Place all in a large cardboard box decorated by the children to resemble a mailbox. A post office "worker" will take all the cards out, place in his or her mailbag (an old shoulder purse) and bring to the sorting table.

Children can be asked ahead of time to bring in Easter Seals, magazine stamps, etc., to paste on each card. Cancel with a rubber stamp.

---

[7] *The Instructor Magazine,* February 1989. Used with permission.

Sort the letters alphabetically according to the recipient's first name. A mail person will put the sorted letters into the mailbag and distribute them by matching the names on the envelopes with the names on the mailbox.

Gloria Needlman Chicago, IL

Appendix H:

Dealing with Diabetes[8]

Dealing
With Diabetes
BY ROBERT NEEDLMAN, M.D.
& GLORIA NEEDLMAN

Q: Amy is the first child with diabetes that I've ever had in my class, and I'm not sure what to expect. Isn't diabetes a pretty serious childhood disease?

The Doctor Responds

Diabetes *is* a serious disease, but with careful management, a child with this condition can enjoy a relatively normal life.

Understanding the causes and treatment of diabetes, as well as related health problems, will help Amy, her parents, and you feel greater peace of mind throughout the year.

Understanding Diabetes

Diabetes occurs when the pancreas makes too little of the hormone *insulin*. Without enough insulin, the body cannot process its primary fuel, *glucose*. Many diabetics require injections of insulin and frequent monitoring of glucose levels through self-administered blood tests.

---

[8] *Early Childhood Today* Magazine, Scholastic Press, October, 1995. Used with permission.

Gather the Facts

Plan to meet with Amy's parents as soon as possible to find out the specifics of her medical treatment. Encourage them to call you if this plan is altered throughout the year.

During your first meeting with parents, note the following:

- dietary restrictions;
- how much physical activity Amy is used to;
- dosage and timing of insulin injections;
- how she appears or behaves just before she is about to become hypoglycemic (see below);
- how she should be treated for hypoglycemia if it occurs in class.

Keep this information in a special folder along with other information about diabetes and the action plan that will be outlined by my mother, below. Review the folder often to refresh your memory.

Know the Warning Signs

Complications of diabetes, like kidney disease, usually don't occur before adulthood, so it's unlikely Amy will experience serious problems while in your class.

You should, however, watch Amy for the signs of hypoglycemia, which occur from time to time after a sudden drop in blood sugar. This usually happens if the child has been overly active, hasn't had enough to eat, or receives too much insulin by mistake.

The early warning signs of hypoglycemia are intense hunger and irritability. Signs of more advanced hypoglycemia include:

- jitteriness
- sweating
- lethargy
- confusion

If Amy experiences hypoglycemia in school, you'll need to follow the treatment indicated by her parents immediately; usually this involves giving the child orange juice or candy to raise the level of glucose in her system.

By educating yourself about diabetes, you've taken an important step towards helping Amy have a healthy and happy year in your classroom.

Tips From Mom

Children will probably notice that Amy is "different" from the very first day. They may want to know why she eats different foods at snack or where she's going when she leaves the classroom for her injections. Include Amy as much as she desires in discussing her medical condition with the rest of the class.

Discuss How Bodies Differ

Review some ways in which people can be different on the outside, then introduce the concept that bodies can be different inside, as well. Explain that sometimes peoples' bodies need different foods and even special medications to work well.

Relate Amy's condition to health problems children already understand, such as allergies. Ask children with allergies to talk about some of the foods they can't eat and the medications they take.

Encourage Amy to talk about her diet and how she takes her medication, then allow time for questions. If children do not address the issue of whether the shots hurt, do so yourself, as this concern is sure to crop up sooner or later. Amy will no doubt reassure her classmates that she can give herself injections in a way that doesn't hurt very much at all.

Finally, because some children may fear this possibility, be sure to emphasize that diabetes, like an allergy, is not contagious.

Prepare an Action Plan

- Add information specific to Amy's treatment to the medical facts about diabetes you've already collected. Here are some guidelines to help you gather more information:

- Find out precisely how often Amy needs to have a snack, since regular food intake is crucial for a child with diabetes.
- Notify family ahead of time about birthday celebrations so they can adjust the child's diet and insulin intake for that day.
- Stock some of the child's favorite foods to substitute for treats she may not be able to eat.
- Keep hard candy or orange juice on hand to treat hypoglycemia.
- Learn from a health professional how to give an insulin injection - just in case.

Your added confidence about handling Amy's condition will help her feel more confident, too.

Robert Needlman, M.D. is assistant professor of pediatrics at Case Western Reserve University in Cleveland, and director of the Continuity Clinic at Rainbow Babies and Childrens Hospital there.

Gloria Needlman has been a teacher at the University of Chicago Lab Schools for over 30 years.

Appendix I:

A Book from a Single Sheet of Paper

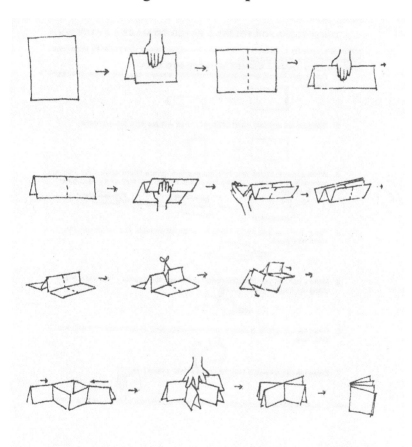

Bibliography for Adults

———•———

Each book offers insightful information worth reading.

Barrett, Muriel and Trevitt, Jane. *Attachment Behavior and the Schoolchild*. Tavistock/Routledge London, 1991

Berlin, I.N. "Mental Health Consultation in Schools as a Means of Communicating Mental Health Principles." *Journal of the American Academy of Child Psychiatry*, 1962

Ekstein, R. and Motto R. L. *From Learning for Love and Love of Learning; Essays on Psychoanalysis and Education*. New York, 1969

Erikson, Erik H. *Childhood and Society*, WW Norton & Co., New York, 1950

Erikson, Erik H. *Insight and Responsibility*. WW Norton & Co., New York, 1964

Field, Kay; Cohler, Bertram; Wool, Glorye. *Learning and Education: Psychoanalytic Perspectives*. International Universities Press, Inc, New York, 1989

Freud, Anna, *Freedom from Want in Early Education*, *The Writings of Anna Freud*, 425-241., International Universities Press, New York 1968

Freud, Anna; *Normality and Pathology in Childhood: Assessments of Development*. International Universities Press, New York, 1965

Furmen, Erna: *What Nursery School Teachers Ask Us About-Psychoanalytic Consultations in Preschools*, International Universities Press, New York, 1986

Hanko, Gerda; *Special Needs in Ordinary Classrooms*, Basil Blackwell, 1988

Kephart, N.C. *The Slow Learner in the Classroom*, Charles E. Merrill 1971

Needlman, Gloria. *A Behavioral Study of Young Children's Involvements in a Hands on Museum.* Chicago, 2003

Piaget, J. *The Origins of Intelligence in Children.* International Universities Press, New York, 1952

Piers, Gerhart and Maria. *Play and Mastery* (and any articles or titles you may find by these exceptional teachers.

Redl, F. *When We Deal With Children*, New York Free Press, 1966

Salzberger-Wittenberg, Isca; Williams, Gianna; and Osborne, Elsie. *The Emotional Experience of Learning and Teaching*, Routledge 1983

Vigotsky, L. *Thought and Language*, MIT Press, Cambridge, 1962

Books Cited in this Book

Mike Mulligan and His Steam Shovel by Virginia Lee Burton; Houghton Mifflin, 1959 *(see p. 21)*.

Worms Eat My Garbage by Mary Appelhof; Flower Press *(see p. 47)*.

The Mouse and the Motorcycle by Beverly Cleary; Wm. Morrow Publisher, 1965 *(see p. 49)*.

The Sorcerer's Apprentice, Disney version or others *(see p. 59)*.

Children and Social Development and Our Connections to Other Species, by Olin Eugene Myers; Westview Press, 1998 *(see p. 63)*.

Significance of Children and Animals by Olin Eugene Myers; Purdue University Press, 2007 *(see p. 63)*.

The Big Friendly Giant by Roald Dahl; Penguin Books, 1982 *(see p. 82)*.

Adventures of Pinocchio by Carlo Collodi *(see p. 8)*.

The Universal Declaration of Human Rights an Adaptation for Children, by Ruth Rocha and Otavio Roth *(see p. 127)*.

Follow the Drinking Gourd, by Jeanette Winter; Dragonfly Books, 1992 (see p. 132).

Chinese New Year Books (see p. 101):
San and the Lucky Money. by Karen Chinn.

The Lion Dancer: Ernie Wan's New Year by Kate Waters and Madeline Solvenz-Low.

Bringing in the New Year by Grace Lin.

The Gift of Time by Dr. Arnold Gessell, Gessell Institute; 1987 (see p. 113).

Lifetimes, The Beautiful Way to Explain Death to Children, by Mellonie & Robert Ingpen. 1983 (see p. 92).

Hospital Books (see p. 107):
Going to the Hospital by Fred Rogers, 1988

Curious George Goes to the Hospital, by A. A. Rey; Houghton Mifflin, 1966

The Day of Ahmid's Secret, by Florence H Perry & Anne Perry Heide; Wm. Morrow, 1990 (see p. 112).

Everything Changes All of the Time, by Morris Philipson ; Harper Row, 1986 (see p. 151).

Read-aloud Chapter Books

Books to read aloud to young children. (Hardly a complete list – many other books to be shared and enjoyed)

The Big Friendly Giant, by Roald Dahl, illus. Quentin Blake, Penguin Press, 1982.

The Boxcar Children, by Gertrude Chandler Warner, Albert Whitman, 1942

Charlotte's Web, by E.B. White, illus. Garth Williams, Harper, 1952

Cricket of Times Square, by George Selden, illus. Garth Williams, Macmillan, 1960

The Dragon of Blueland. by Ruth Stiles Garnett, Scholastic Press, 1951

Elmer and the Dragon, by Ruth Stiles Garnett, Scholastic Press, 1950

Mouse and the Motorcycle. by Beverly Cleary, Scholastic Press, 1965

My Father's Dragon, by Ruth Stiles Garnett, Random House, 1948

Adventures of Pinocchio, by Carlo Colladi, Puffin Classics, 1940

Pippi Longstockings, by Astrid Lindran, Puffin Books, 1945

Ramona, by Beverly Cleary, Harper Collins, 1955

The Universal Declaration of Human Rights, Children's Adaptation,
by Ruth Rocha, United Nations, 1955